LEARNING COMES OF AGE

LEARNING
COMES OF AGE

....

JOHN WALKER POWELL

....

Published for the Adult Education Association
of the United States of America by
ASSOCIATION PRESS, NEW YORK

The preparation and publication
of this book were made possible by the
assistance of the Fund for Adult Education

Library of Congress catalog card number: 56-10661

⬤⬤⬤ 55

Printed in the United States of America
American Book–Stratford Press, Inc., New York

In the belief that only a vigorous, informed, and democratically vigilant people can remain free—

In the recognition that among a free people, learning for every citizen must be a process continuing throughout life—

In the understanding that the capacity to perfect skills, to enrich living, and to increase social understanding and effectiveness is ever present in human beings—

In the knowledge that adults through education must seek continuously new and better ways to achieve these ends and ideals—

We, who share these convictions, seek to build a stronger adult education movement through this Association.

—Preamble to the Constitution
of the Adult Education
Association of the U.S.A.

Preface

This book came into existence at the invitation, and at the expense, of the Adult Education Association of the U.S.A. and the Fund for Adult Education. It was intended to be a general survey of the present state and future prospects of adult education in this country. But it is characteristic of its sponsors that they left the writer completely free to develop the study in his own fashion, and to write what he saw and thought. In fact, the agreement was one that expresses the ideal relationship between writer and sponsor: I was to write it as I wished, and they didn't have to print it if they didn't wish.

In actual practice, however, there has been wide and valuable collaboration in the writing. First, it is based on scores of recent visits and conversations across the country. Second, it draws heavily on the increasingly mature and thoughtful literature of the field, from the days of Morse Cartwright and the American Association for Adult Education, beginning in the mid-twenties, to the present. Third, the manuscript, at three stages of revision, has been carefully read by members of the AEA's Publications Committee, from whom I have had many wise and helpful suggestions. In some considerable degree, therefore, the book represents what "we" think, rather than merely what I think.

This collaboration is important for another reason, too. From about 1950 to 1955, I was engaged in researches outside the arena of adult teaching: in group research; in research for the improvement of medical education; in field studies of community response to disaster; and in the practical politics of city and state organization for mental health. After this busy vacation, I return to adult education as a student of the field, rather than an actor in it. I hope this will produce some advantages in freshness and objectivity of perspective. I know it has enabled me to accept with admiration and gratitude the gifts of knowledge and experience which my collaborators have offered me.

Now a word of explanation, and a few notes of appreciation:

The main topic of this book is adult learning. Of course learning, the exercise and discipline of intelligence, goes on all the time, in countless moments of many people's experience. Every time you discover a new quality in an old acquaintance, new beauty in an old picture, new meanings in an old book, new revelations about your old self, you have learned, you have given your intelligence something new to work with and to work on. But these are accidental, unorganized events. Turning raw experience into learning is perhaps man's most exciting activity; but we can't deal with random learning in a planned and purposive way. Education must be provided for, or it can't be counted on.

So, in this book, I shall restrict terms like "adult education" to mean *planned and purposive adult learning occasions regularly provided under some organized scheme of guidance*. And the chief sources of information, for the immediate purpose, will be the studies carried on by several major educational organizations between 1951 and 1953 at the request of, and with funds provided by, the Fund for Adult Education, an independent organization established by the Ford Foundation. These studies were as follows:

American Library Association:

Adult Education Activities in Public Libraries, by Helen Lyman Smith. Chicago, 1954.

American Management Association:

Management Education for Itself and Its Employees. New York, 1954.
Part I, *Management Education in American Business,* by Lyndall F. Urwick.
Part II, *A Survey of Management Development,* by Joseph M. Trickett.
Part III, *Case Studies in Management Development,* by Robert G. Simpson.
Part IV, *The Education of Employees: A Status Report,* by Douglas Williams and Stanley Peterfreund.

Association of Land-Grant Colleges and Universities:

Rural Social Systems and Adult Education, by Charles P. Loomis et al. East Lansing, Michigan, 1953.

Council of National Organizations of the Adult Education Association:

Adult Education: A Directory of National Organizations Represented in the Council of National Organizations of the Adult Education Association. New York, 1954.

National Education Association of the United States, Division of Adult Education Service:

A Study of Urban Public School Adult Education Programs of the United States. Washington, 1952.

National Social Welfare Assembly:

Young People and Citizenship, by Edward B. Olds and Eric Josephson. New York, 1953.

National University Extension Association:

University Extension in the United States. John R. Morton, director. University of Alabama, 1953.

Union Education Survey. Mark Starr, director. Reprinted from *Labor and Nation,* Fall, 1951.

In addition, I have made frequent use of several books already in the field: some of the "Studies in the Social Significance of Adult Education in the United States," issued by the old American Association for Adult Education in the thirties, especially those by the Overstreets, Alvin Johnson, and Bertrand Meland. I have also used several of the newer studies: Robert Gard's modest and passionate account of *Grassroots Theater* (University of Wisconsin Press, 1955); C. Hartley Grattan's amazing feat of compressing a comprehensive history of adult education into a very readable account of men *In Quest of Knowledge* (Association Press, 1955); Malcolm Knowles's wise and informative *Informal Adult Education* (Association Press, 1950); and the encyclopedic Sheats, Jayne, and Spence *Adult Education* (The Dryden Press, 1953). I was also given food for thought by Carl F. Kraenzel's *The Great Plains in Transition* (University of Oklahoma Press, 1955).

Among my interim correspondents, I would give full credit to the perceptive and thoughtful contributions of Robertson Sillars, Editor of Publications for the AEA; Robert Blakely, manager of the Central Regional Office of the Fund for Adult Education; Eleanor Coit, director of the American Labor Education Service; Thomas Van Sant, director of Adult Education for the Baltimore Public Schools; Lois McCarthy, executive secretary of the Council of National Organizations; George Fern, of the National Association of Manufacturers; Ellis H. Woolley, of the American Society of Training Directors; and, of the AEA Publications Committee, these members: Arthur P. Crabtree, Bureau of Adult Education, State Education Department, Albany, N.Y.; John C. Glidewell, of the Public Health Department of St. Louis County; Harry L. Miller, assistant director of the Center for the Study of Liberal Education for Adults; Leo Molinaro, executive secretary of the Adult Education Foundation of Akron;

James Rietmulder, director of Association Press; Robert H. Schacht, of the University of Wisconsin Extension Division; and Grace T. Stevenson, of the American Library Association.

My gratitude to all those whom I visited in 1955, who answered my questions and argued with my postulates and joined in the attempt to clarify and put into words this tremendous thing we all believe in so deeply and comprehend so inadequately, cannot be put into a catalog. I should like to think that this book itself was its expression.

For the opportunity to write the book, to act as spokesman for a movement, and for the freedom to make myself one of its interpreters, I am deeply grateful. It is, I know, a high privilege. It is also, I must add, a responsibility such as only the foolhardy would undertake. Indeed, I have with difficulty resisted the impulse to dedicate this volume

> *To all those in Adult Education*
> *who were my friends and colleagues*
> *until I wrote this book about them.*

Acknowledgments

Some of the best fun I had was in finding quotations to head the different chapters; and these authors I count among those of my friends who helped me say what wanted to be said. My thanks are also, of course, due to their publishers: to Longmans, Green and Company for the quotation from Mary Follett's *The New State;* to Diarmuid Russell for permission to quote from AE's *The National Being;* to Alfred A. Knopf, Inc., for the passage from de Tocqueville's *Democracy in America;* to Henry Holt and Company for the passage from Robert Frost's *Complete Poems,* the bit from "The Death of the Hired Man" (copyright 1930, 1949, by Henry Holt and Company; copyright 1936, 1948, by Robert Frost); to the Oxford University Press for the passage from Christopher Fry's *The Lady's Not for Burning* (copyright 1949, 1950, by Oxford University Press); to The Macmillan Company for selections from A. N. Whitehead's *Adventure of Ideas,* and for the use of the delightful quotation of Johann Sebastian Bach from Albert Schweitzer's *J. S. Bach,* trans. by Ernest Newman, 1950; to Oscar Hammerstein II for the lines from *The King and I* (copyright 1951 by Richard Rodgers and Oscar Hammerstein II; Williamson Music, Inc., owner of publication and allied rights); and to Brandt & Brandt for use of the excerpt from E. E. Cummings' poem from *Poems, 1923–1954,* Harcourt, Brace & Company (copyright 1950 by E. E. Cummings).

J. W. P.

Contents

Part Four: TOWARD A STRUCTURE FOR ADULT
EDUCATION

Part Five: TOWARD A PHILOSOPHY OF ADULT
EDUCATION

LEARNING COMES OF AGE

Part One

AIMS OF ADULT LEARNING

CHAPTER 1 *Introduces the Reader, the Author, and the Theme*

> Figured bass . . . is executed with both hands in such a manner that the left hand plays the notes that are written, while the right adds consonances and dissonances thereto. . . . Like all music, the figured bass should have no other end and aim than the glory of God and the recreation of the soul; where this is not kept in mind there is no true music, but only an infernal clamor and ranting.
> —Johann Sebastian Bach

WHEN YOU pick up a book and glance into it, as you are doing now, you are shaking hands with an author. The book is to be a conversation between your mind and his. You want to know whether he has anything interesting to say, and what he wants from you in return.

Like all conversations, this one is apt to go a bit better if we know a little about each other before we start. I already know a few things about you. You read, you look into books, you have curiosity of mind. Second, the fact that you picked up a book with this one's title suggests a further fact: that you are interested in learning, in education. You may be a student, or a teacher; you may be a program director, a board member, a librarian, a company executive, a member of a study group. But you care about education—and so do I.

What I care most about is *adult* education: that is, how

3

you and I, now that we are grown up, can go on learning
how to make our living both satisfying and significant.
My side of this conversation, then, will be about adult
needs, and ways of meeting them; and about the needs
of the adult education movement itself, and how it can
come fully of age.

On one hand, I shall try to describe briefly what is
going on in this field of endeavor, playing the notes as
written; and the other will add consonances and dissonances thereto: consonances to emphasize the newer and
more significant trends that might become break-through
points into new avenues of growth; dissonances when I
come upon things I think you or I or the workers in the
field are dissatisfied with, or ought to be. I shall seek to
avoid any infernal clamor and ranting.

The theme is the adult, with his stake in the world
and his desire for the mastery and the enjoyment of life.
The variations are the life-tasks he is concerned with, the
ways he has of learning how to put his concern into
action, the ways in which learning can help him find out
who he is and how he stands among his people. And I
want also to try to define some of the issues of growth
that confront the movement for adult education: the need
for a fully adult method and subject matter, for a stable
institutional form, for a recognizable profession, for a
new art of combining multiple agencies and organizations
and volunteer citizens into a comprehensive educational
pattern that will help America itself come of age. I am
very much in earnest about this; and I think the time is
past for pulling our punches.

So who am I, that I should write this book? Well, at fifty,
I have been more than twenty years in adult education.
My specialty is book reading-discussion groups, about
which I have written some books and articles; and I am
primarily a group man, though I have done other sorts
of teaching too. I taught philosophy to undergraduates

in one university, and education to graduate students in another. I have worked on the staffs of public libraries and of mental hospitals, doing education in both. I have organized and chaired an Adult Education Council, and done a lot of conference and workshop duty. I have taught in University Extension, and I have done adult community education in rural areas. I have done educational broadcasting on radio and television. I have been president of a state Mental Health Association, and have done work with the YWCA, the League of Women Voters, and the P.T.A. I have been a union delegate to two city Labor Councils. I grew up in Duluth and Minneapolis and Madison, in Ohio and Florida and New England and California and North Carolina; my children were born in San Francisco and grew up in Arizona and Washington, D.C., and Baltimore.

Furthermore, I have just completed an automobile tour of eleven thousand miles over twenty-eight states, stopping to talk with all manner of adult education leaders in all sizes of cities and towns, trying to find out what was going on, what was important, what was needed. This book, then, comes out of all of that: all of my own experience and all that I talked over with the people active in the field. So it is not just my book. Any of a number of other people could write it, and it would say nearly the same things. This has to be true, or the book isn't.

Now let's consider this astonishing young giant industry—the provision of planned learning for the mature years.

CHAPTER 2 *Looks at the Growth in Adult*
Learning Activities

What's one and one and one and one and one
and one. . . ?

—The White Queen

Up THE SIDE of our kitchen doorframes
there has always run a series of pencil lines, with initials
and dates: the fond record of the children's stature as
they grew. We are all enamored of statistics in eras of
expansion. Americans love to record the growth in the
number of automobiles and telephones and stockholders,
of wheat acreage and factory output.

We have developed statistical procedures to a high
point: proportions of the population can be predicted
for those who will ride streetcars, who will read books,
who will be struck by lightning or inherit fortunes.
Science's grasp on the universe consists chiefly of calculated probabilities; and our own grasp on America is
largely in terms of a quite mad variety of probabilities
affecting fractions of the American population. One wonders if E PLURIBUS UNUM should now be retranslated as
"One out of [every so] many."

Among the welter of recorded changes there are a number that are significant for our purpose. Massive changes have taken place, within quite recent years, in the proportions of older adults within our total population; of high school and college graduates in our population; in the number of leisure hours available to adult Americans; in the proportion of skilled and technical jobs and requirements in business, industry, and agriculture. Perhaps largely in response to these changes, the number of people in their mature years who are engaged in some form of learning activity has also increased massively.

Statistical claims in this area are notoriously unreliable, however, for a variety of reasons. One is that the definitions of "adult education" are loose and all-inclusive; those who define it have no wish to step on the toes of any of their colleagues, however collateral their relationship.

The latest responsible estimate of total figures is that by Malcolm Knowles, administrative co-ordinator of the Adult Education Association of the U.S.A. He prefaces it with these comments: "For statistical purposes, the definition of adult education is limited to continuous (as against sporadic) experiences organized specifically for the purpose of adult learning. Even with the definition narrowed to this extent it is practically impossible to obtain reliable statistics. . . . Attendance rosters are kept for relatively few adult education activities, and no systematic method for reporting enrollments exists." Public school adult programs that collect money on the basis of average daily attendance, of course, are very methodical indeed; but few of the rest of us can resist the temptation to make the program look good, or at least a little better, when we make our retrospective estimates of informal attendance. At any event, here is Knowles's comparison of present estimates with those made by earlier scholars:

Estimated Participation in Adult Education

	1924	1934	1950	1955
Agricultural Extension	5,000,000	6,000,000	7,000,000	8,684,000
Public School Adult Education Programs	1,000,000	1,500,000	3,000,000	3,500,000
University Extension and Evening College Programs	200,000	300,000	500,000	1,500,000
Private Correspondence Schools	2,000,000	1,000,000	1,000,000	1,000,000
Educational Radio and Television	500,000	5,000,000	6,000,000	5,000,000
Library Adult Education	200,000	1,000,000	1,500,000	1,961,000
Men's and Women's Clubs	1,000,000	1,000,000		1,525,000
Parent-Teacher Association	15,000	60,000		350,000
Religious Institutions	150,000	200,000		15,500,000
Business and Industry	100,000	50,000		750,000
Labor Unions	30,000	15,000		850,000
Armed Forces Educational Programs			250,000	388,500
Health and Welfare Agencies				6,500,000
Others	4,681,500	6,156,000	10,000,000	2,000,000
Total	14,881,500	22,311,000	29,250,000	49,508,500

"These estimates," Knowles adds, "do not take into account the fact that some individuals may participate in more than one type of activity. Even so, they indicate that probably more than a third of all adult citizens will participate in some form of organized educational activity in 1955, tripling the volume since 1924."

A third of America's adults enrolled or enlisted in some educational program? This is not true of my own acquaintance, overweighted as it is on the educational side; is it of yours?

The figures are misleading, as Knowles says, because we count one set of things and take them to represent another. We count registrations and attendances, ignoring the fact that the same person may appear several times in one table. We have not studied the amount of overlap: people who use the library, belong to study groups, take extension courses, and participate in church educational programs, for example.

Above all, we have been afraid to separate some activities from others and limit the term "educational" to them. A typing course; a week-end workshop on community theater; a talk to a Grange by a returning traveler; a university lecture on mental health; a session with a librarian on what to read to improve one's vocabulary; a church school lesson; a study session of the League of Women Voters; a correspondence course; a talk to a Parent-Teacher group; a book review before a Homemakers' Club; a semester course in Humanities at a local college: all these are counted as equivalent units of educational activity.

Yet if we take single indicators, such as adult enrollment in day and evening colleges, the trend which Knowles suggests is apparently quite real. In growing numbers of junior, state, and community colleges, the adult enrollment already outnumbers the undergraduate. Up to 30 per cent annual increases in adult registration are noted in recent years. University Extension Divisions which not long ago relied on part-time services from campus professors now have their own full-time academic departmental faculties.

Public school adult enrollment has not kept pace with the colleges, except in some cities where the evening program is specifically and frankly adult rather than remedial. Chiefly, this fact reflects the increase in college population, and what I like to call Powell's Third Law— that adults in general will not go back to a school on a level which their own schooling has passed. Much of the adult college enrollment, of course, consists of high school graduates going on to college at night; but a growing proportion of the college-level courses is *non*-credit, also.

If it is true that the rise in college graduates corresponds with the increase in continued college-level study, this suggests that our colleges have been doing a good job of inculcating a taste for study, and of bringing to reality the old adult educators' maxim that "in education, Commencement is only the beginning."

But let's take a look at the other side of the figures, too. The "educationally inert" population is also huge. Hundreds of towns are without a public library, and millions of adults make no use of the libraries that are there. Every year tens of thousands drop off the educational ladder, at anywhere from the fourth grade to the Ph.D., and we have no way to find out how many of them ever get back on.

What, then, is the "adult education population"?

In evening colleges and other more formal occasions, largely concerned with advancing formal course training, the population is primarily young adults, probably concentrating between ages 25 and 30. But in informal education, ranging all the way from civic and social organizations, community development groups, and farm and labor organizations on the one side, to library groups, book groups, forums, liberal study and arts groups, residential campus institutes, leader-training workshops, evening school hobby and practical arts courses, parent education groups, University Extension groups on adult subjects, and the whole gamut of adult learning activities, on the other side, a rather unexpected and quite significant coincidence emerges: there *is* an adult learning population with a vaguely recognizable social profile. Its main features are these:

The clients of adult learning are mostly 35 or older. Two-thirds are women. Most of these people live in cities and larger towns, have incomes between three and eight thousand dollars, have from one to three children in school. They are people with relatively stable homes,

steady jobs, and a little better than high school education on the average, but ranging through graduate degrees. They tend to be the busy people, rather than the
idle ones. Most people who appear in one adult learning
occasion have been, or are, participants in others, and
will continue to be. Characteristically, they confess some
concern for events, and some liking for people; they tend
to be rather verbal, and to be readers at least of newspapers and periodicals: the home that is totally bare of
print reflects a life that is usually barren of any attempt
to understand itself.

In age, economic status, and pattern of social activity,
the population I have described is the one that has probably increased in size faster than any other major segment of our people, during the last two decades. The
increase in their enrollment in adult education, then, is
partly a simple result of this growth in the educational
consumer group. It is outside this group, among the rank-
and-file labor and farm workers, and among top executives, that adult education has its hardest struggles with
promotion. Within this consumer group, education is in a
seller's market. It reflects less credit on the offerings of
the purveyors than on the motivations of those who take
whatever learning they can find. Those of us who plan
for adult education have been riding on a cushion. Our
numbers have grown. The question is, have *we?*

CHAPTER 3 *Suggests Some Major Areas of Adult Concern*

> No policy can succeed if it be not in accord
> with national character. If I have misjudged
> that, what is written here is vain.
> —AE, *The National Being*

> There seems to be little time for ignorance.
> —Eleanor Roosevelt

Y ES, WE in adult education *are* growing up.
In its youth, the movement responded to necessities:
schooling for those who had not gone long enough to
school; Americanization for those who joined our population late; vocational training and retraining for those
we needed in our factories. Between the feet of these
massive necessities, like early mammals scampering
among the saurians, ran the predecessors of truly adult
study forms which would develop later: Lyceums, study
clubs, Chatauquas, reading clubs. Out of these, in recent
years, has grown a broadening recognition of adult learning's real job—the provision of learning opportunities for
the *adult mind as such;* and of learning not just how to
do what must be done, but also better ways of *being*
what we are.

Helen Everett Meiklejohn tells of being with a bus
load of Welsh coal miners on their way to a labor meet-
12

ing. It was a long bus ride, and on the way they sang (being Welsh), and they talked poetry and recited poems. She says they knew the New England poets better than she did. Now, did this make them "better" coal miners? Of course, they had also studied labor economics, and political science, in their union and Workers' Education classes. What did this make them better at?

The confusion between Being and Doing, between the person and his vocation, has plagued all discussions of education. One man will stay in the mines, and become an educated coal miner. Another will take a course in bookkeeping, get a job in an office, and turn from an uneducated miner to an uneducated bookkeeper. We usually call both these processes "education," with the result that we seldom know what we are talking about.

The grown person has many vocations: those to which he is "called" to *earn* his living; those which he chooses as ways of enjoying being alive; those in which he has to discharge certain responsibilities to his fellows, as a family man or as a citizen, and to enjoy his relationships with those companions of his living. But ants and bees and microscopic parasites also perform their tasks; they mastered "doing" long before Man did. But we have no idea what "being" may mean for them: the experience of sharing life with companions, of serving known purposes, of choosing and enjoying. Nor have we much concern about that; we, the latest masters of life on this planet, are still concerned with our own discovery, whose intoxication was expressed by Sir Charles Sherrington, the great British physiologist, in his Gifford Lectures at Edinburgh. "The Universe," he wrote, is "heroic background for what to us is an intimate and an heroic epic. A birth in cataclysm. Aeons of seething and momentous shaping. A triple scum of rock and tide and vapour—the planet's side—swept on through day and night. Then from that side arising shape after shape, past fancy. And latterly

among them some imbued with sense and thought. And
still more latterly, some with thought eager for 'moral
values.' The planet, furnace of molten rocks and metals,
now yielding thoughts and 'values'! . . . All that counts
in life. Desire, zest, truth, love, knowledge, 'values,' and,
seeking metaphor to eke out expression, hell's depth and
heaven's utmost height. . . . We live at a moment hitherto
unmatched, for our planet has just evolved mind in us
to the pitch that we can take in our local situation of
this present as we walk her side. Mind, yoked with life,
how varied in its reaction! It will sit down and watch
life acquiescent, or on the other hand take life and
squeeze it like an orange." [1]

Mind is a product of life; and living, at least for men,
is shaped in turn by the way they put their minds to
work upon it. Thinking is another of Man's vocations; it,
too, is a form of doing. But there still is a difference in
our meanings when we think of *the thing being done* and
of *the person doing it.* In *doing,* a man is an instrument, a skilled and specialized tool, serving a purpose. As
person, it is he who has the purpose, who chooses that
this shall be done and in this way. These are, if you like,
the realms of know-how and know-why. Know-how has
been America's specialty, as has the schooling that pro-
duces it. Our need, now in maturity, is in the other realm,
in the development of ourselves as persons rather than
as instruments. And this, to me, is the realm of education.

I say "to me," but I mean also to a growing number
of those who plan for education in maturity. This recognition is, in fact, one of three reasons why I say that
adult education is itself beginning to come of age.

A second is the even wider recognition that the achievement of maturity through education is a never-ending
process. Our language habits had trapped us into making

[1] Sir Charles Sherrington, *Man on His Nature* (New York: Cambridge
University Press, 1951).

education into a noun, a thing. You either "had" an education or you hadn't, or you went somewhere to "get
one." In times of profound unrest and concern over our
economy or our country's role in the world, "educated"
adults would say to us in San Francisco or Washington,
when we proposed group readings of Veblen and Smith
or of Beard or Toynbee, "Oh, I don't need economics, I
don't need history; I *had* them in college." You would
have thought history was a form of measles. But the discovery that has become accepted throughout the adult
field is that educating oneself is a process, not a package.
The goal is not to acquire a set of ideas but to maintain
the power of the thinking muscles, to keep the *process*
of understanding ever alert.

The key recognition of all, finally, is that there is an
adult mind, different from those of the youth and the
undergraduate; that the grownup has a qualitatively different way of using his mind, of relating ideas to experience, of weighing and using knowledge. It is for this
distinctively grown-up mind that education in maturity is
now, increasingly, being planned.

Our universities had a taste of this difference when the
GI's came back from World War II and from Korea.
Where the usual undergraduate had only his expectations of adult life, the GI had had experience of it. Where
the undergraduate was still facing the choice of a mate
and a vocation, many of the GI's had made theirs, had
cast the dice and taken responsibility for the outcome.
The University of Maryland Medical School, when I was
working there in the early fifties, was having the novel
experience of teaching pediatrics to students with children of their own. Other colleges were teaching sociology
to students who lived in complex trailer communities and
were working at their own community problems. Unhappily, the undergraduate courses themselves were left
unchanged; the students from the trailer slums were

taught in terms of the problems of people who lived back of the Yards in Chicago. But the experience with older students, even though that tide has receded, has left its watermark on many teachers; and it suggests some of the differences that adult education is coming to recognize in its own clientele.

Recent research in what is called "human development" has also been highlighting some of the major differences between the tasks faced by the individual at different stages of his living: in the tasks, and in his performance of them. Out of these studies there emerges a sort of theory about the Seven Ages of Man in American society. The first three decades are largely taken up with getting accepted as a grown-up member of the society: getting his schooling, finding his vocation, finding a mate and building a nest. It is not until he is over 30 that the usual American has time to take breath, to take stock, to look around him for help in learning the tasks he faces next. The children are still in school, the house is not paid for, the head of the household is a very junior executive in his job. In the forties, things change. The children are taking their own memberships in a wider society; the vocation is more securely held; the nature of the marriage is changing, the grandparents need more help, living is at a different pace. There is time, and need, for asking questions.

The next decade faces new kinds of decision. The children are getting launched; the vocation is expert, and individuals are respected in their grasp of it; they have memberships and positions in community organizations carrying more active responsibility; they are being eyed as successors to the retiring, and will soon pass from parenthood to grandparenthood. And the prospect of reaching retirement and old age is becoming an uncomfortable reality instead of a statistical possibility. In the seventh decade, it will take place, along with other kinds of new experience, enjoyable or uncomfortable, but all of it wanting interpretation and help in understanding.

It is not by accident, therefore, that the statistical norm for *entrance* into voluntary adult learning is at about age 35. For by this age, the accumulated changes in circumstances of living have added up to a qualitative change in the personality needs. The man or woman of 35 has at least three points of difference from the youth. He has had *experience* of living as a responsible member of the adult world; he has fashioned a *situation* in which his responsibilities are well defined; and he has solidified some phases of the *self-knowledge,* or at least the *self-picture,* which will govern his actions from now on.

Education now means an enlightening of this experience, an interpretation and evaluation of these responsibilities, an enlarging and deepening of his self-understanding. He seeks now not teachers but companions in the search for greater wisdom. Where the undergraduate grasps at new ideas for the sake of liberating himself from his childhood stereotypes and limitations, the adult grasps at ideas as illuminating what he is already doing and committed to do. This suggests, in fact, a very important difference between the meanings of "liberal" education for undergraduate and for adult—important, and illustrated by our thesis.

What we call adult education is made up both of schooling and of this other kind of learning. For schooling can continue throughout life; there is no age, apparently, at which we lose the ability to take on new skills. And "education," in the sense of the search for understanding, can begin very early: perhaps at the moment when a child first asks himself, "Who am I?"

So the difference is not merely in the age. More pertinently, it is in the curriculum, and in the needs on which it is built. For schooling, the core curriculum was always the three R's—reading, 'riting, and 'rithmetic—with their

accompanying languages and tools. The goal of schooling
is *competence*, at whatever age it is sought.

For this other kind of education, we might describe the
curriculum in terms of three C's: Curiosity, Creativeness,
and Comprehension.

If you think of these three C's as they operate naturally
in children, they will not need much explanation. And
also you will notice how different they are from the three
R's. The saddest fact about our schooling is the uniform-
ity with which it kills, in children, the three C's. In our
mature years, then, we have to leave time and provide
opportunity for them to re-emerge. They are the substance
of adult intelligence.

Curiosity is a motive, creativeness a process, comprehension a goal. There is joy in each of them, and together they make up most of the enjoyment of living.
They all involve judgment, discrimination, decision-
making; and "judgment" is our common synonym for
intelligence, decision our test of its rightness. And all of
these apply in all of the life-tasks we perform as adults.

Many students of our society have tried to define the
"life-tasks of the adult," the roles he is called upon to
perform. To me, this language of sociological abstraction
seems to have an unhappy way of leaving out the living-
ness, the personalness, of the experiences it is describing.
"Tasks" and "performance" have the ring of grim duty;
but being a member of a family, or a man working at his
job, or a citizen excited over an issue like racial integration, these are really just huge swatches of a man's living,
full of fascination and feeling and fury and fun. I should
rather describe these major areas of our living as constellations of relationship with other people, and as
realms of value-choice and action-choice. They involve
ambition and striving, and frustrations and problems, and
problem-solving and satisfactions. From the individual's

point of view, perhaps the best single word for these areas of "task" and "role" is the old Quaker word, *concern*. When someone in a Friends' meeting says he "has a concern," it means that he has a live and urgent interest in a matter he believes important and wants something done about.

The American in his lifetime has very many concerns. But, as adult, they can be seen as clustering around a few major constellations of concern: his membership in a community, in a family, in a vocation; and the arts of enjoying the world he lives in, and of having good relationships with others. The language we use in talking about these concerns will depend on whether we are thinking about them from inside the individual, or as the individual is seen and measured by outside observers. He himself approaches these concerns with *expectancy;* the people around him impose on him a set of *expectations,* which is quite another matter. He sees himself as trying to *be* good at these jobs; others see him as *doing* well or badly in them. Parenthood, to him, is an experience to be enjoyed and understood; from without, it is a role to which certain quantitative measures of success and failure might be applied. He wants his living to be admirable and enjoyable; others scrutinize it to see whether it is successful.

I am not saying that these two points of view are in contradiction, or even in conflict. One finds familiar expression in novels, plays, and poetry; the other in sociology and history. One seems to lay stress on being, the other on doing. But both are valid—so long as they do not forget about each other. Both are involved in all our major areas of adult concern. Because each area does involve roles that must be performed, it calls for competence in the appropriate skills. Because it involves us in relationships with others, it requires comprehension. Because it calls for choices of values and actions, it requires creativity. And because it demands knowledge, it appeals to curiosity. On the other hand, because each is a major field of activity within an organized society, society has developed certain institutions, regularized patterns or ways of organizing men's behavior within each cluster of interests—the family, for instance, with all its connections to institutions of marriage, of property, of name and succession, of law and right and obligation. And finally, because things change, each of these fields of activity is also subject to changes: the family is beset by changes in living and housing patterns, by increasing longevity of its older members, by the growth of professional services like schools and health and recreation and welfare; modes and mores in marriage and child-rearing became altered; and the whole field is subject to the stresses between forces trying to keep it as it was and forces tending to alter it toward a new pattern.

Oh, yes, indeed; these major clusters of our adult concern and performance are no rote tasks to be taught. They are small universes calling for the utmost intelligence each of us can muster. This fact has led educators into the trap of planning for what people "need," as though understanding were a vitamin pill. All I am trying to point out here is that these concerns are areas in which people are already using their intelligence, and *want* to understand better than they do. What is my evidence for this rash assumption?

The evidence against me is considerable. Much of our reading is trash. Most of our conversation is trivial. And— here is an extraordinary fact that dawned on me only recently—never in any American novel or story or play that I have read does any character take any time to seek education about the problems the novelist has involved him in: from Hawthorne to O'Hara, our writers see us as people with consuming problems and no urge to get help in understanding them. In terms of Malcolm Knowles's figures, the one-third of a nation that engages in adult learning has thus far failed to include, or at least to attract the notice of, its literary spokesmen.

It is only as you get the American engaged in serious conversation that his underlying desires begin to be revealed. In years of working with adult students I have come to believe that the American does a lot of private thinking (which he is shy about revealing) on the subjects of his concern: his country, his community, his neighbors; his parents, his children, and his relationships as child of one and parent of the other; his relation to, and his destiny in, the universe; his private interests and hobbies; his friendships and enmities, and his successes and failures in getting along with people and in understanding himself. The interest is there. But many a latent citizen is discouraged about acting because he feels powerless to affect the course of events; and many a potential student remains inert because he feels diffident about "exposing his ignorance" or about his ability to manage a book or contribute to a discussion. Education's problem is that of invitation, motivation, the giving of success-experiences in its occasions; and this is what much of our conversation, in this book, will be concerned with.

Objectively, too, we Americans make strong claims to our interests in the five fields I mentioned as major constellations. In three of these, we make utterance of pride, not always equalled by our performance. In two of them, we demonstrate our interest by our actions while denying it in our words. The first three are *democracy,* our pride in ourselves as citizens capable of handling the stupendous task of self-government; the *family,* our sacred belief in the essential human group; and the *job,* our pride in know-how, in running (even though we may not have invented) machines and vocations and organizations better than any other civilization. The fourth is the *enrichment of living,* about which we speak only with a kind of embarrassed jocularity: we, who buy and play more fine records than people in any other country, speak scornfully of the Longhair; who are a major world market for good writing, make fun of the Highbrow; who paint, design, weave, sing, dance, and create, pretend either that these are folk-practices too quaint for serious notice, or else that they bring good money, so why shouldn't we? The fifth realm is that of human relationships, of *self-understanding*, about which we are sometimes pretty nervous: we, the most psychiatrically oriented and served nation on earth, jam our magazines with jokes about witch doctors and head-shrinkers, yet privately confess our fears about emotional stability, our doubts about our capacity to love or be loved, our questionings about the reach and reality of human values.

These concerns, because they comprise many of the deepest interests of our people, can therefore be thought of as suggesting a sort of "core" for an adult *curriculum.* This is a hard word to define. After years of making up sequences of books for adult groups to read, I came to the conclusion that a curriculum is a set of learnings so intimately related to each other that *each* of them seems to be prerequisite to *all* of them. And this *is* the intimacy of relation among our five fields of interest. For each of them is in reality a set of relations with other people; and whichever set you start to think about, one of the others will seem to need understanding first. This is what leads men into becoming specialists; and the relationships among their specialties sketch the profile of a program for adult learning.

Let's look at these areas, now, a little more carefully. At the periphery, so to speak, are the questions and obligations involved in being a member of a community that is part of a nation which is working at its role among a world of nations. The mature American is a householder; he votes, locally, statewise, and nationally; he is a producer and a consumer; and he is likely to be involved in some movement or organization to advance the welfare of the community or the nation or the world of mankind, along some particular line. In being all these, he wants to understand our own history, to have available what Van Wyck Brooks called "a usable past." He has to think about politics, and about the nature and problems of our economic system—and about those of other nations as well. He is called on to make choices—informed ones, if possible—about local and national policies on a myriad issues. His choices involve guesses about world conditions, about the international currency in human values, and about how our own actions affect the world and vice versa, including the effect of other countries' actions on the security of his own community. Law and the Constitution and how laws are made and how courts interpret them are necessary parts of his understanding. He has to reckon with the urbanization of American culture as opposed to the agrarian cultures of our neighbors; and to have some acquaintance with the alien practices of other folk, their customs and ways of thinking and languages and literature. He cares also, however, about slums and schools and tax rates and traffic and sidewalks and police and insurance rates in his home town. In short, this is the area in which the individual handles the web of threads that link him to his city, the nation, and the world.

It is in this area that he throws around such terms as "freedom," "rights," "interests." It is here he wants to know whether his own thoughts and actions can affect local matters, national issues, world affairs. Here he is also subjected to a barrage of expectations levied on him by other people, by friends and party and press and union and club. In this area, you see, he acts not solely as "citizen"; he acts in response to his interest also as parent, as worker, as philosopher of history and society

—whether he would recognize himself in that description or not.

The area of family membership is even more intimately pressing. Growing to independence; making a marriage; making a home; raising children: familiar goals and roles, pressed by motivations from within and expectations from without, shot through with dubious choices that never end. The role of child, for example, begins as a relation of dependence, goes through a long struggle for independence, and ends by taking care of dependent parents. Before this is completed, the child has had children of his own who go from dependence toward independence; and he must look forward to his own renewed dependency. These are tough transitions to make. It is hard, for example, to accept dependence on one whom we still think of as dependent on us: one of our family's favorite stories is of the 93-year-old neighbor who said to her 70-year-old daughter who was starting upstairs carrying a lamp, "Clara Lyon Peters, give me that lamp! You know you're not old enough to carry it up those stairs."

Growing up, as anyone in a family can tell you, is largely a matter of meeting the expectations of other people. And families fall easily into what Hollywood calls "type casting": you get known in one kind of role, and it's hard to break out of it because people go on expecting you to be that again. It's not easy to keep our expectations of a child geared to what the child is really *ready* to be. Here is where we need curiosity, about the real person in the child; creativeness, in making circumstances that bring that person out of the type-cast child; and comprehension of what the process means, why it is important, and what our own role in it is.

But society, too, falls into type-casting. As the child emerges from his family into wider relations with the community around him, this bigger family is likely to have certain stereotyped roles ready for him: he can be delinquent, athletic, artistic, a hot-rodder, a square, and a few other things; and the adolescent must try to find a role for himself among these recognized types—while still trying both to maintain and to shake off the role of child in his own home. This is not an easy time. We've tried to improve it by centering our attention at the high school level of training, to get the adolescent to meet his tasks better. We have to supplement that by adult use of the three C's, to play our own parts better.

Besides all this, we ourselves as adults accept certain roles, do our own type-casting: "Every child that is born into this world alive/Is either a little Liberal or else a little Conservative." I am—that is, I see myself as—a Good Citizen, a Good Father, a Good Sport, a Pillar of the Church, a Scoffing Skeptic, a Hard Worker, or something of the sort. What happens is that *we stop thinking*, turn off our curiosity and creativeness and comprehension, because the chosen role has certain thoughts expected of it, certain behavior imbedded in it, certain values embodied in it, furnished for it. It's like moving into a furnished house and adopting its taste as our own.

Now look at the changes in the life-tasks as we face old age. Society has a certain album of expected types of Old Person. Some are friendly, some are dreadful; but all consist of sets of expectations, which are embodied in our actual provisions for the aged. In our social picture, old people are expected to be home-dwelling dependents. Turns out instead that they prefer to live alone and keep working at something. We think old people should be glad to lay down the burden of work. Turns out that retirement is our number one man killer in the mid-sixties. Medical miracles can prolong life threatened by illness; but no one has yet found the cure for retirement. It takes curiosity about the *real* conditions of satisfactory aging, finding out instead of just expecting the familiar stereotype. It will take the creation of massive new habits, perhaps new technologies, as well as the wide spread of creative activities; and it takes a great deal of comprehending. We pay attention to our schools so that our children can have a better shake than we did. But we must pay attention to aging, for our own sakes.

The "tasks" that cluster around our vocations are not simple: skills on the job, and skill in relating our own job to the larger enterprise of which it is a part; trade memberships, perhaps expressed through unions or professional organizations, involving the need to understand the meaning and purpose of the trade we're in, and our own role in it and contribution to it; and many threads of relationship to fellow workers, to employers, to employees, to the consuming public.

Here, you are in the role of Wage Earner, about which society has many notions. The particular job you've learned to do further defines your role: we have varying sets of expectations about, say, lawyers and plumbers. But the outstanding change today is taking place in industrial employment. Today's assembly line, meeting orders for cars in dozens of individual color combinations and assortments of accessories, is far from the one that turned a single nut on an endless line of Model A's. The rapid introduction of technological miracles, electronic controls and the like, is calling for a rapid re-education of large sections of the labor force. Management, too, has recognized new needs and demands; the development of replacements for present management has become a major field of education in the last ten years, with universities and adult education agencies increasingly involved. And, significantly, what management is looking for turns out to be the development of men with curiosity, creativeness, and comprehension. A good head of an accounting department is not, they find, automatically a good vicepresident or president. Training is not enough; education is required. Labor union executives, another kind of Management, are coming to the same findings. I don't mean to suggest the millennium; and there are immense problems of democratic participation left unsolved in both areas. All I mean to say is that the earning task, the role of worker, is changing at such a rate that the old stereotypes will not suffice any longer to guide our expectations about it.

From the periphery of social membership we have worked our way in to the individual himself, first in his knowledge and enjoyment of his relation to his world, and finally in his understanding of his relation to his fellows. While the first of these takes in an infinite territory, to me its chief feature is the enjoyment of living, the enrichment of life—the realm of play, so to speak, as against the sober realms of obligation. In this area I, myself, would include the intellectual pursuits, as well as the arts. Here too, I would include religion, both as philosophy and as worship; for it, like the arts, is an affirmation of ourselves in relation to the universe: the affirmation that the universe is capable of intimate response to me, and I to it.

The other realm, the last of the suggested five comprehensive ones, I call the realm of self-understanding. I choose the self as focus, though I mean to include all efforts to comprehend human beings and human relations and the curious ways of mankind; for in all my study of other people, the object I am searching for is myself. But "I" am elusive. There seem to be several of me, and some of me want what others of me fear, some of me approve what makes others of me angry, and each of me finds some reflection of itself in the other people I live among, work among, and read about. I am a little Society, a group—in short, a human being. All of my life I shall, like others of my kind, be trying to discover the ways in which I correspond to the society of my fellows, and it to me. For

here, again, I am met by the expectations of others, by
their notions of what I am or ought to be, even by my
own picture, borrowed from them, of what I am and
what I ought to be.

In all these major areas of adult relation and performance, my "task" is confused both by my many roles and
by the stress between old and new demands—my own
upon myself and others upon me. Without the freedom
to search, and the effort to learn, I could still fall into
easy slavery to those demands, into acquiescence in stereotyped roles. Unless education, at adult levels, helps us
to focus our minds on these problems of task and role,
we may suffer more and more from the lag between our
expectations, our old stereotypes based on what used to
be, and our new realities. Left to itself, society might
even freeze all roles into a set of expectations from which
no one could break free. Look at the primitive tribe:
there your schooling is simply your growing up into accepted tribesmanship. Everyone is your teacher. There
are solid skills to learn, like fishing and sago cultivation
and pottery making. There are prescribed roles which you
have to learn because you are born into them: Older Son,
Mother's Uncle, Head of Household, Important Man, and
a hundred others. Each one has its prescribed ways of
acting in relation to all the rest: these two must insult
each other; these two may not speak; and so on. When
you have mastered them, you are accepted as a Person,
one of Our Kind. (In many primitive languages, the word
for their own tribe and for Human is the same: if you
aren't one, you aren't quite the other.)

Ours, however, is a loose-jointed society, full of diver-
sity and contradictions. But it is also knit together by the
interrelations between the realms of adult action, and
among the institutions that try to govern these. The "citizen" is a working family member; the "worker" is a voting
family member; the family head is a worker and commu-

nity member; and in all three roles he is also a person who has opinions, makes judgments, approves some values over others, and tries to understand himself and his neighbors—and his enemies. If "institutions" became rigid, we too would become a monolithic society; it has happened to other great nations in our time. The whole measure of a *free* society is that it plays by rules that keep the players—as ballplayers say—"loose." The coach is not dictating every play; the function of individual judgment is still paramount. Therefore, the only true mark of a free society is that it provides to its members the opportunity to keep their minds active, their information objective, their communications open: in a word, *education.*

We have been discussing education in relation to the principal "roles" that the mature American has to play, and to the problems that arise within and among these roles. Now the question is: Is there a field of knowledge that we can acquire in order to solve all these fluid dilemmas? What *super*-role does society offer us, to resolve all the rest under one kind of mastery? Is there a schooling for this?

There is a schooling for each role; but that is where the danger lies. To be sensitive to many roles, to be able to make *appropriate* judgments about them and about the roles of other people, takes something different. Usually, we just call it *intelligence.*

Intelligence, not knowledge, is the aim of education. Rather, it is the subject of education, the material it works on; for intelligence is an activity, a muscle, an organ of sensitiveness. Knowledge can't be transferred from field to field: your ability to plot an end-around play on the football field won't help you much with mathematics; your knowledge of chess is little help in learning bridge. But intelligence, as Dr. Flexner wrote in a book on education many years ago, is "capable of being applied in any field whatever." A man may be an *intelligent* student of social questions, music, and baseball. Or, he may just have opinions about them, stereotypes like "longhair" and "red" and a distaste for men who chew tobacco.

Now the job of education, it seems to me, is that of keeping intelligence so alert, so tuned to many pitches of experience, so sensitive to other people and other ideas and other ways, that its possessor can live in many worlds at once, and be at home in all of them. He can make judgments with his feelings, as well as with his mind, that are appropriate to the subject. He may not be a civic leader, or a performer in organized activities; but he can at least be an intelligent spectator; and every team, including the Congress of the United States, plays better to an informed gallery.

Most important, intelligence is not a *collection* of skills. Intelligence is YOU thinking, making judgments about and in the course of and among your different roles and realms of action. Your intelligence is the guarantee that you are *one* person, after all. "At the center of his multiple memberships stands the individual himself. Where all the lines of training intersect, there is a person." At the core of your many selves, there is "the Watcher, the Witness."

You see why this is so important for our conversation. Knowledge and skill will serve each of our concerns; but education has to center on the person himself whose living is fulfilled through all the realms he lives in: on his intelligence, his discrimination and judgment and richness of resource and maturity of decision. We need schooling, so that we can do what we must. We seek education, so that we can be what we will.

Part Two

AGENCIES OF ADULT LEARNING

Chapter 4 Discusses the Principal Agencies
of Adult Learning

Chapter 5 Discusses Associations and Councils

Chapter 6 Denies that the Present Patterns Are
Adequate

CHAPTER 4 *Discusses the Principal Agencies of Adult Learning*

> To recognize the community principle in every-
> thing we do should be our aim, never to work
> with individuals as individuals. . . . Every de-
> cision of the future is to be based not on my
> needs or yours, nor on a compromise between
> them nor an addition of them, but on the rec-
> ognition of the community between us.
> —Mary Parker Follett, *The New State*

As I CRISSCROSSED the country in the sum-
mer of 1955, from Boston to Los Angeles, from Louisville
to Minneapolis, from Denver to Phoenix, I was also quar-
tering the fields of adult program activity—those covered
in the Fund for Adult Education studies, and others not
yet studied. I visited libraries, labor education workshops,
evening schools, community colleges, training directors'
meetings, management associations, community arts centers, extension centers, and centers for liberal adult study.
And from all the educators I talked with, in cities and
towns, one clear strong note was dominant: the frontier of
adult learning is moving ahead, it is breaking new ground.

The statistical bulk of adult registrations is still in the
area of schooling: vocational and upgrading and credit
courses. But the educators themselves are thinking beyond this point. The vast job of *schooling* is well in hand,

hugely organized, enlisting more and more resources of college and university, high school and junior college, university extension and agricultural extension, industrial training and training in union skills, technical and hobby schools and libraries. The attention of the educators, meanwhile, has moved on to what now seem more pressing urges: the urge to liberal adult learning, to the enlightenment of men about their community problems, about their personal values, about the great world of ideas and arts.

In terms of method, the emphasis is shifting steadily away from the classroom and toward the group. This is significant, because schooling serves mainly the goals of *individuals*. The emerging pattern of education is *an attempt to bring people closer together, on broader grounds of common interest, with higher standards of intellectual search for a deeper understanding of their common goals.* The emphasis is therefore swinging from "transmission" in the direction of widened *communication*, with all its implications for method, content, and organization. And, in a significant proportion of cases, this is coming about through a livelier interaction of each agency with the *community* that surrounds it.

Let's take a look first at the familiar institutions of learning: libraries, schools, colleges, universities, and extension services. These agencies, professionally staffed and administered, account for about a third of the enrollment, and more than a third of the personnel, involved in adult learning. Traditionally, their excellence has been judged by their success in helping individuals increase their powers. This was the basis on which they began offering their educational services to adults. What I am suggesting is that in recent years their programs, goals, and conception of their role are being transformed by the experience of getting actively involved with the adult community, and finding its values and its vitality infusing their service.

Libraries

It is easy to see the Public Library as an educational institution because its business is books, and books are the prime nourishment of learning. But a loaf uneaten is not nourishment, and a book unread is just a pound of paper. Education, in libraries as elsewhere, is an activity, the active provision of a program of opportunities for learning.

The library is not educational because it has books in it. It is educational in precisely the same terms as other institutions: in terms of what it provides and encourages in the way of learning. Therefore it must be examined in the same terms as other institutions, though with it always understood that, as a library, it may have special learnings appropriate to its general function.

It might be hard to say what those learnings are, however, in a library that shows movies, makes radio broadcasts, gives record concerts, lets clubs meet in its smoking room, posts booklists, leads reading-discussion groups, and circulates books and periodicals. These same functions are also performed, respectively, by museums and churches; radio stations and schools; radio stations and music clubs; churches and public halls; civic organizations and churches; university and volunteer groups; and extension divisions and rental libraries. What's so special about the library doing them?

Nothing special, really. But the library recognizes that it *is* an institution for education, and has long worked at finding out how to be, as it is sometimes called, "A University for the People." Beginning with advice to individuals who want "something to read," it moved years ago into "Readers' Advisory Service" that actually helped people plan programs of self-education. The readers' advisers began working with groups, as well as individuals;

and groups began asking libraries for programs and leaders. By 1945 there were some libraries that organized
and conducted reading groups of their own. By 1951, the
American Library Association (one of the first champions
of adult education through reading, back after the first
World War) had a national program going in many libraries, its own American Heritage Program of book discussion, financed by the Fund for Adult Education. Local
libraries were also beginning to use programs from other
sources, such as "Great Books" and the "package" programs of the Fund for Adult Education.

Over the same period, especially since 1940, libraries
moved into the field of visual education, beginning to
stock as well as show movies and filmstrips for discussion,
and helping groups and organizations to plan and present
picture material. Music listening had long been provided
by libraries with record collections; and here again there
has been growth in active provision for programming and
for learning by discussion and related reading.

There are two ways in which the library has special, if
not unique, functions as an education center. It alone
keeps available the most possible of the best possible
materials from all fields of learning and creativity: books,
music, art, things that are at once the result and the
source of creative experience. Universities tend to specialize in what they collect. Libraries have a more universal
responsibility—and that in an expanding universe. Second, the library is probably the only true neutral ground
in any community. It is not committed to a doctrine or
to a membership, like churches and clubs; its rooms are
not dedicated to proprietary interests, like lodges and
political halls. And because we can come and go at our
pleasure in libraries, it is more relaxed, more truly open
to the community, than the public school.

It is, therefore, altogether right and proper for libraries
to undertake active exploitation of the materials they

house. In doing so, the library is properly eclectic in its approach: it seeks and accepts both students and teachers from any and all legitimate sources, uses all manner of materials, and professes no creed or object except the increase of sensitivity, knowledge, and use of intelligence among the community's people. It uses whatever methods it knows, or that the leaders whom it borrows from other sources know.

One of the frequent activities of libraries is arranging book exhibits and displays, and educational exhibits related to the aims of other organizations and meetings. Another frequent service is to act as a clearinghouse and information center for adult education activities around the community. Libraries also take part in co-operative program planning with other agencies and in interagency conferences on materials, methods, planning, and leader training. A speaker looking for a film on his subject can come to the library and look at what it has; in some libraries he can ask to have his audience come there to see and discuss it.

Increasingly, libraries in larger cities are providing their own programs of book discussion, film and music discussion, public affairs lectures, mental health film series for parent groups at branches, and a variety of other educational events. These meetings usually are led by individuals recruited from outside the library, and often planned with outside professional help. There are, in short, two ways of library programming: that which is done to help other agencies at their request, and that which the library initiates and gets others to help with.

The basic function of the library is still that of *getting people to use books*. To this end there are two means: promotion and invitation. By *promotion* I mean getting books out into places where they will be used, but where they would not have been used unless the library brought them there. In the words of Harold Roth, of the East

Orange Public Library, "We have found that the residents of a community are usually unable to define the exact type of service that will satisfy their needs until they are shown that they can get it. The library, therefore, works on the basis of carrying on a continuing demonstration of the variety of activities which are available." That library, for example, places book collections in hotels and churches, and has special services for shut-ins. In many states, bookmobiles promote the use of books in rural areas. And few librarians miss the chance, when they are collaborating with someone else's educational program, to put out books and bibliographies at every meeting.

Invitation, in its pure sense, is a matter of creating *easier access* to books. The most dramatic innovations here are in architecture and in technological tools. There has been a genuine break-through in recent library architecture. Perish the Carnegie pile of stone; in its place stand symphonies of brick and glass, classically modern, lavish with color, flooded with light. To name a few examples I know myself, the new main buildings in Providence and Phoenix and Cincinnati, the new branch buildings in Akron and Baltimore and New York and Detroit, are a delight to the eye and an invitation to the mind. Inside, shelves are open and easy of access. The very arrangement of *things* explains to the visitor that the librarian is a helper with books, not a guardian of them. The new smoking-browsing lounge at the Enoch Pratt Free Library in Baltimore is always filled with comfortable people. (I cherish the memory of one scene there: a sign, READ, SMOKE, RELAX; and beside it, in an easy chair, book on his lap and dead cigarette in his fingers, a man fast asleep.)

Access through technology has been dramatically attempted by the public library in Louisville. But here a curious problem arises. The new tools of the twentieth century, in the field of learning, are what we call the audio-visual: radio, records, tape, movies, television. Only one marked advance is possible in dealing with books as such, and that is the micro-card, which permits enormous collections to be housed in a small space, and read by means of an enlarger. Louisville promotes this device; but its major emphasis has been on the creation of massive archives of taped music and radio programs, of records and films. Programs made from these materials are broadcast to the schools, and to the public. A network of leased wires can carry record and tape programs directly to listeners in branch libraries, and even into the psychiatric ward of the local hospital. You can come to the main library and take away, on your card, books, movies, fine reproductions of great paintings from Greco to Dufy— even an umbrella to keep them from the rain. But the point is that you don't have to come to "the main" to enjoy the use of its archives. You step into your neighborhood branch, ask the librarian to request a tape to be played for you at the main library, and you sit in the branch with earphones and hear it. This service keeps a bank of forty tape reproducers busy in the basement of the main building; but high school students can operate the machinery, and the maintenance costs are very low, while access is very broad. Louisville, like other libraries, is eager to have other organizations make use of its films and services; and for some years the University of Louisville has joined in the movement toward easy access by putting non-credit liberal courses, under its own instructors, into the library branches to make them "neighborhood colleges."

Other libraries, of course, are also adjusting to twentieth-century tools. Stuart Sherman in Providence had two television setups built into the new main building, with coaxial cables to the Telephone Company, against the time when the library could begin telecasting promotional and educational programs. The Enoch Pratt Library joined with the Walters Art Gallery and a TV network in a series of telecasts on the historical background of notable books, including Shakespeare and Marco Polo. Others have undertaken comparable adventures; and the public library is always, so far as I know, one of the backers of Educational Television wherever a local organization for this purpose exists. So, in sum, the library has not "outgrown" its reliance on books; but its promotional and invitational resources have been vastly strengthened by the addition of non-print materials.

The characteristic result is a trend toward a combination of invitation and promotion, through multi-method programs initiated by and held in libraries. Here are six evenings of "films for parents" in neighborhood branches, with teachers to lead discussion and librarians to present reviews of related books. There, offerings in branches include American Heritage reading-discussion (which may be enhanced by records or films or pictures) of de Tocqueville, Thoreau, Lincoln, Twain, Sandburg, and others; Great Books reading groups; a series on Basic American Freedoms; a series on modern art, using films, books, and discussion. Lectures in the library, art and handicraft exhibits, recorded music evenings—all these devices are used to invite people into the company of books.

In these attempts to respond to existing demands and to create new ones, the library has never abandoned its original aim: to get more people to make better use of better books. This effort, which is part of every librarian's daily routine, has in fact been behind these new programs; and it has been increasingly focused into adult educational terms. The American Library Association has a growing Adult Education Section, and an Office for Adult Education. And out of these has come the culmination of its experiments with adult concerns: The

Library-Community Project, another FAE-financed activity.

I call it a culmination because I think it is the result of a recognition that all the group programs and many of the individual client problems of libraries have their real source in the community of adult concerns. It has been interaction with community groups and interests that has sparked the new additions to "librarianship" and forced the inclusion of adult education content in professional library training. This has happened despite the opposition of many librarians, and more trustees, who have argued that education is not the library's business: "Let the schools and colleges do their job, and the library confine itself to its." This is a real issue, and very much alive. But the rising tide of adult learning has carried the library with it, and the vanguardists within it have responded with imagination and courage, with new tools and new ways of studying the library's role. And today, with national backing, state library leadership, and local library participation, the interaction of library and the adult community is under active investigation in four states, with immediate concrete results in local understanding and practice, and a long-range promise of a vital re-education for the library itself.

Public Schools

Public school adult education, especially at the high school level, is more than other institutions bound by the set of public expectations built up in a proud record of over a hundred years of adult teaching. But the significant fact in the FAE study of 1951–52 seems to me to be the large number of cities that were *recommending changes* in the emphasis and role of their evening high school adult work.

As of 1951, a quarter of enrollees were workers, a quarter housewives with high school educations, on the whole;

one in twenty was of professional rank. Subject choices favored vocational and avocational skills and business; but there had been marked increases since 1946 in such areas as driver education, physical education, and civic affairs. Parent education was moving up, as were fine arts. But Americanization, which was one of the first great charges laid upon these schools, still ranked high in 1951, as did regular academic high school subjects. To quote Louis Mather's summary of the Public Schools study, over the five-year period of general expansion in adult enrollment "the gain in cultural studies [arts, academic, and Americanization] was almost negligible, in vocational activities very moderate, and in the area of social skills very great indeed. The public affairs groups, which more than quadrupled on an average (including cities of all sizes) tend to emphasize the trend shown by the social skills activities. It is a picture of 'Social Man' replacing 'Economic Man.' . . . Even though the pace in some [small] cities may be slow, the same changes away from vocational training and toward social skills and Public Affairs are seen everywhere. General academic education seems to have been left in a backwater, as shown by trends in enrollment of students." More and more public school adult education directors have become involved in helping parents solve immediate practical neighborhood problems, and hence in the growth of "community development" programs outside the curriculum and beyond the school grounds.

Related changes are taking place in method. Three fourths of the enrollment in 1951 was in classroom, demonstration-laboratory, and informal group courses. But "the formal lecture shows the greatest reduction in popularity over the five-year period. Correspondence courses, which can be considered 'frozen' lectures, are also going out of fashion in one city out of four. . . . These methods limit individual participation to an absolute minimum, and the adult school student of today wants to play an active role" in "activities which allow him a considerable measure of self-expression. The forums, panel and informal group discussions, and demonstration-laboratory methods give him an opportunity to join actively in the learning process. Where these informal methods are used, [even] the most academic studies are attracting students. Plato's *Dialogues* can be studied by informal discussion methods by students who would drop out of an old-fashioned straight lecture and home-study reading class."

It is apparent in the study that the increase of public affairs and civic interest enrollment is directly related to the growth of collaboration between the school and various groups in the community: international affairs groups like the United Nations Association or United World Federalists; labor unions and business and industrial firms; women's clubs and veterans' organizations. The enrollment in public affairs forums, for example, falls into an average attendance of about 125 per meeting, but meetings may be fewer, and the initiative may have come from an interested organization in the town. This may account for the discrepancy between the large increase in public affairs enrollment in large cities and the lack of significant increase in cities under, say, 50,000.

It is in the area of collaboration with other organizations, also, that the wistful emphasis on change appears in the discrepancy between present facts and recommended movement. Part of the Public Schools survey consisted of self-surveys conducted by local committees interested in community adult education. Graphs (see *A Study of Urban Public School Adult Education Programs*, pages 105–107, 109–112) suggest the trends in leadership thinking within the respondent cities: thinking about drawing educational leadership from non-school sources; about giving leadership to non-school organizations;

about extending adult programs beyond school buildings; about making school facilities available to more adult activities; and about the community as a source of program content, and as a collaborator in further self-study.

The conclusion I draw is that even here in the very stronghold of pure schooling, the present trend of thinking is moving ahead toward *community integration* in the collaborative study of common areas of concern; and this by adult means, rather than by traditional school methods. New York State evening schools in rural towns have become dynamic centers of community political discussion in a broad and rapidly growing program designed, in Arthur Crabtree's penetrating phrase, "to Americanize the *native*-born." [1] New examples of public school–university collaboration in several states, Michigan for one example, promise the development of school activities in the direction of a more thoughtfully perceived community role and function.

Our schools still face the handicaps of inadequate finance and inadequate training of personnel for adult service: in 1951, adult programs received only two cents for every dollar spent on school children in the same cities. But their growing importance in the affairs of the *adult* community could be the key that unlocks the vaults of community support.

Community Colleges

Beyond the high school, the junior colleges have also been pressed into the service of the rising adult tide. In the locally controlled junior colleges reporting in the survey, the average adult enrollment ran around five hundred a year, with a somewhat higher proportion of people with more years of education and higher occupational and income status than are reported for evening high

[1] "Adults Keep Up with the Times," *National Education Association Journal*, February, 1954.

schools. Here again, however, the subject emphasis is on vocational and business courses, which with practical arts and crafts make up over half the junior college adult enrollment. Exceptions here are individual: some junior colleges carry more cultural responsibility than others, like Santa Rosa with its Great Books program, or San Bernardino with its active community education program.

As the evening school and junior college move in the direction of becoming "community schools," they too will find major changes taking place in their curricula and methods, perhaps in their structure—and their personnel, most of whom at present are trained only in the instruction of the young. Somewhat similar changes are taking place in many of our state colleges—only a few years ago they were two-year normal schools; now an increasing number are four-year general colleges, and take on the character, and sometimes the name, of "Community College." San Francisco State College, for example: in 1950 its enrollment was 90 per cent in teacher training. In 1955, only half of its courses were in education, and under exceptional leadership it had joined hands with many groups in the community. For various social welfare agencies it trained workers and volunteers in dealing with the handicapped. It gave apprentice training to workers for thirty-six children's agencies. For business groups it had offerings in world trade and in insurance; it was moving into the areas of employee training and executive development; through an off-campus center it provided workshop experience for city school personnel. Its fine arts facilities were used by adults, with or without credit, in art and music and drama. It had undertaken a research project in finding college graduates who had not worked in public schools and giving them direct trial experience in teaching under expert supervision, to see whether new people could be attracted to teaching by this kind of "reaching back" into the community. Nor

is this development at San Francisco State unique among
state colleges; many others could duplicate the story, and
add to it.

All these institutions are moving, too, toward providing service to special population groups, of whom perhaps the "aging" are the most familiar current example.
"Groping" would be more accurate than "moving," here,
since none of us yet knows what the real needs are and
how best to satisfy them. But as we do learn, the schools
will find their functions and methods changing still further, their role within the community still further altered.

A very real qualification of the proposal to make the
college serve "the community" is enforced by the fact
that many college and small university facilities cannot
be afforded on the basis of the home-town attendance
alone. The "community" which an active college serves is
likely to be the state and the region. Ohio University, at
Athens, for example, finds itself serving several different
kinds of "community" with its special institutes and workshops for adults. When there is a well-known artist in
residence, for two weeks of painting, the students come
from many states; and similarly with musicians in short-
term residence. The Executive Development workshop
draws from industries outside of Ohio. Perhaps only the
Theater Arts and community theater really serve townspeople along with undergraduates, without drawing from
very great distances. This is undoubtedly true for all
college-community theaters, such as those at Oberlin,
Antioch, and many other small colleges. But play production, band concerts, and lectures on campus continue to
serve, and to enlist and involve, the adult population
lucky enough to live in a college town.

Another service of the college to the small community
is exemplified by Earlham College, at Richmond, Indiana. The Community Dynamics program, originally developed to add a realistic dimension to undergraduate

learning, follows an action pattern not unlike that of the American Friends Service Committee, Earlham being a college in the Friends' tradition. The program brings small numbers of faculty and students into actual working contact with groups and committees in small towns near Richmond (or as remote as Puerto Rico), where they help the townspeople identify and study some community problem—recreation, getting a new school, forming a health committee; whatever the town itself feels the need of. The college group then serves as a kind of volunteer staff, always on the town's invitation and under its direction: staffing the playground, keeping the minutes, or whatever is appropriate. The community goal is the development of local leadership and skill in getting things done for the town. Back of such programs, of course, lies the tremendous pioneer work of Jess and Jean Ogden in community development for the University of Virginia Extension Division; and beside it loom the massive community development programs of large Extension Divisions like those of Michigan and Wisconsin. Methods vary from one institution to another, as does the amount of direct leadership or guidance given by the professionals. But the essential motive is the same in all: to help people learn that they can do things about their town, and learn how to do them for themselves.

The comment that rises to mind at this point may seem irrelevant; but I shall come back to it later on. It is this: that the Earlham undergraduates, in this joint experience, are having *a planned educational experience to which their other studies are related.* Are the townsmen?

Evening Colleges

At the head of the community adult college ladder stands the University Evening College, of which there are now enough to man a national association. At this moment, the evening college is stretched upon a Procrustean bed, undecided whether to ask adults to tailor their habits to undergraduate standards, or to widen the range of college practices to fit the different requirements of the adult student. In some evening colleges the "day school" program is reoffered at night, under the day school dean. Others have established separate evening curricula under separate deans. In both cases, there is evidence of strain in the attempt to serve two masters.

Some of these university evening colleges have a long and respectable history. The University of Cincinnati, for example, began its adult service some fifty years ago. But today's stresses are reflected in them, too. In a traditional setup, such as that of McCoy Evening College of the Johns Hopkins University in Baltimore, 1955–56 enrollment showed a sharp rise in numbers, especially in engineering, business, and education—based, in Dean Mumma's opinion, on "the desire to improve job efficiency," "the critical shortage of scientifically trained personnel," and "the wish to keep ahead of, or abreast of, the constantly rising level of formal education of the American people." Almost a third of the evening students already hold a bachelor's degree. By far the largest number of courses are given for credit, though some students do not plan to use the credits. But there are some non-credit courses; and there is a small but steady demand for courses in philosophy, the arts, music, literature, and world studies in culture and social history. It is also significant that numbers of the evening students are sent in by their employers, some of whom refund the tuition when the course is completed, others using payroll-deduction plans for installment buying of added schooling, and still others holding out hopes of promotion based on successful completion of certain types of study. Probably over 10 per cent of McCoy students are there under employers' incentive plans.

In a pioneer vanguard stands a subsidized experiment at Brooklyn College, to try to evaluate the experience and self-education of adult students in the awarding of college degrees and to modify the college methods of teaching to fit the "advanced standing" of the superior adult student. After careful screening, thirty-two candidates were selected for the trial; and it is very interesting to note that, on "area" tests devised by the College Testing Service, these adults, without college education, scored *above* the average of several thousand upper-level college sophomores and seniors in both social science and humanities learning, and did not trail by far in the sciences. A further result of this experiment has been a staff attempt to develop materials and procedures especially adapted to the desires of adults for learning in broad fields of interest.

Annual conferences of representatives of the University Evening Colleges, sponsored by the Center for the Study of Liberal Education for Adults (which in turn is supported by the Fund for Adult Education), are helping to clarify the role of this widely spread urban agency in adult learning. It is not too early to say that here, again, live interaction with the local community is the vital determinant in shifting content and procedures in a fully adult direction. In some cases the age group served is younger than the average in adult programs, and in these and other cases the motivation for study appears still to be individual advancement. I am not decrying this motive. But I suspect that an inquiry would show that those university evening colleges that *have* tried to mesh gears with the ongoing adult forces in community life would show a greater than average advance in the direction of fully adult approaches to learning, more thoughtful awareness of the meanings of the roles which the adult student plays within his community.

University Extension

The agency that serves all levels of student, as well as all parts of its state-wide area, is the University Extension Division, whose clientele, though wide-ranging, represents on the average a higher age bracket, higher schooling level, and higher income bracket than those on the high school and junior college adult levels. Here are the professionals: teachers, doctors, engineers. Here is management, including union management. But here, too, are the mute inglorious Miltons, enlisted now in creative writing and theater arts and music. And here, in at least a dozen states from Pennsylvania to California, are the resources for community self-development with university help.

University Extension, to paraphrase a recent song title, is a many-serviced thing. It seeks to make campus courses available to people who cannot reach the campus. It may maintain off-campus centers for the first two years of college. It may create a Continuation Center, pioneered at Minnesota, to which professionals from all fields can come for intensive short courses and institutes in recent developments within their own fields of expertness. It can offer non-credit courses to adult students in far-scattered towns. It can offer leader-training courses for organizations throughout a state. It can set up summer institutes and workshops for workers, for industry, for school teachers and administrators. It can run a library extension service, sending packaged reading materials to client groups out over the state. It usually does some instruction by correspondence.

It is called adult education because all of its services are available to grownups as well as to undergraduates. But the ways in which it steps frankly out into the arena of adult living, to meet adults on their own level and with their own problems, are more difficult to define.

One of these ways is of course the professional Continuation Center, which has been called "the graduate school of adult education." Another is community development services, which attempt to help people as members of a community dealing with its needs, rather than as individuals seeking advanced schooling for themselves. A third way, less widespread but of real significance as a university adult service, is typified by the Wisconsin Idea Theater and Rural Writers' Conference.

The roots of this program, particularly in community music, reach back in Wisconsin for at least four decades. Today, the annual Community Arts Workshop, in summer residence on the Madison campus, integrates four well-staffed state-wide services: in theater, with some thirty community groups; in creative writing, with 2,200 members enrolled in the Rural Writers' Conference; in art, with an itinerant artist-in-residence furnished by the Division of Agricultural Extension in the University; and in music. The participants are sometimes school teachers in these fields. More often, they are men and women of considerable maturity, from the small cities and towns throughout the state.

"The leaves of glory hung over the giant cities, but the roots of creativity lay in the towns a thousand miles away," writes Julius Landau in a moving account of the Workshop. "The towns watered the roots with legend and song and young genius who left early and took all legend. The town harvested the pale flickering shadows on their movie screen and the hollow laughter of their radio. Now the towns are watering the roots of art for a local harvest of legend and song and story. The leaves of glory hang over a soft summer night's concert in the park, an art show in the library. . . .

"The Workshop moved away from the metropolis and the emphasis returned to the original dream, a workshop for *community* arts, arts in the home, the church, the community theater, the civic orchestra, the city chorus, the local painting show; community arts in the prairie, creation in the streets, creation in the local halls; community arts, a private creation, a song during seeding, a poem in the kitchen, a story while the lathes are still, a painting by a window. . . .

"Learning, teaching, uncovering the fragile fibre of shy creation, a logging song, a three-page play, a poem scratched on a brown paper bag. . . .

"There is a hang-over of non-respectability about art in many communities. People who paint don't tell. Then when a local art show is announced, the whole town is surprised at the great number of entries." [2]

Reading this, you remember what an ancient and honorable tradition this is within our culture. Painting and music have been part of America's towns as long as the Bible, almost. The womenfolk were responsible for the painting and the literature; but the men sang, and played in the band. How many small towns are without their bandstand? When the Mormons left Ohio for Utah, they kept their bands playing, for pleasure and profit, all along the weary road; and the Community Recreation Building, with a theater, was one of the first that Brigham Young had built.

The point of this is that all these folks—like my uncle who led the band in Mankato, Minnesota, and could play all the instruments in it—were amateurs. The man plays because *amat:* "he loves." There is considerable authority behind the theory that a lot of music poorly played for love of it is healthier for a nation than ten superb orchestras and a hundred and sixty million listeners.

Further, while there is class feeling and possessive feeling to divide the different groups that follow different branches of the amateur arts, they are in essence parts

[2] "A Report on the Third Annual Community Arts Workshop," University of Wisconsin Extension Division, 1954. (mimeo)

of a whole, and feed each other: writing, scene design and painting, acting, and all forms of music go into Theater. The wealth of the classic theater is as available as the struggling pages of the local playwright. Theater has been greatest in countries where the whole people were audience, and everybody wrote a little. The unexpected excellence of writing and production of short dramas on television has, I believe, inspired and released a new generation of creators and lookers, who feed each other; and I think America's theater is due for an increase in stature. But Hollywood and New York City are still, as in a sense all markets are, the enemies of the ultimate producers. The people cannot rest on them; they must rest on the people.

Every kind of educational content can be integrated with the arts, and gain by being presented in unexpected fashions. The early Soviets taught the virtues of toothbrushes through touring companies of players. The National Association for Mental Health circulates plays that local groups can put on and discuss to their own greater enlightenment. College theater and young people's creative dramatics groups are tremendously increased recently. According to Edward Kamarck, of the Wisconsin Idea Theater staff, 1,437 community theater plays and 28,000 school and college plays were presented in 1953, beside the 4-H and other groups that acted too; and in Wisconsin alone "there is more [theatrical] activity than there was in Elizabethan England."

In short, I think there is a clue here to one of the essential characteristics of true adult education. It is the furnishing of enthusiastic professional guidance to the creative efforts of the adult amateur who is, in the end, the substance and the carrier of the culture. But the requirement of creativeness goes far beyond the arts alone. Our thinking about communities and societies, our decision-making, our relations with other human beings, all require a creative sensibility which cannot be taught by rote nor learned from lectures. Not only the great advances but even the little break-throughs in daily life are made by a creative sensitivity to the novel elements, the individual factors, the risky possibilities, in the actual situation. This can, in a sense, be learned. That is, educational practice can emphasize situations in which people develop their sensitivity and their courage. In the most significant instances, these situations arise within the *community of adult concern*. It is for this reason that I would judge the arts and community development services to be the *most* fully adult programs within the gamut of University Extension; and the community-centered programs of the Extension Divisions to be the most fully adult influences upon their own further growth.

Resident Adult Centers

Now, I have dinned upon this cymbal of "the community" until my reader may feel deaf in that ear, or think that I can hear only on that side and must be deaf on the side of the individual's need to withdraw from action and engage in more private and independent contemplation of his living. If I had meant this, I should have been false to the way I myself live, and believe people should live. Libraries and reading groups and campuses are truly withdrawing-places, where we can catch our breath and gain some perspective on the struggle into which we return. For adults, at least; for here again we see the difference between "preparation" for living and *enhancement* of living. The withdrawing-place must contain real nourishment; we go to it as the giant Antaeus touched earth, to refresh our vitality. It is only when these places weaken and cheapen us, or encourage us to widen the gap of our privacy from those with whom we work face to face, elbow to elbow, that they are warped from their educational function.

In support of this, I would point now to the growth of residence centers for adults: to the campus centers for short-term group courses and conferences; to the week-end conference centers, on and off campus; to colleges like Goddard, that devote much of their free campus time to adult seminars; to the summer short-courses-in-residence that are becoming an ever larger feature of the adult-serving institutions; to the growing number of labor's residential courses and conferences; to folk schools like the Highlander Folk School, in which European precedents are adapted to American uses.

Among experiments in education for being old, one with potential significance is the Cold Spring Institute, up the Hudson River in New York State, to which groups of men and women over sixty are invited for a year of rediscovering the skills of health and hobbies, and to reconsider who and what they choose to be for the rest of their lives. The struggle with retirement is, in our society, as real as the struggle for adult competence; and, like the latter, it too has to be self-directed, but with the help of thoughtfully planned opportunities to face the new problems and acquire the new wisdom. Brought down from the mountaintop and adapted to urban resources, the concept of a withdrawal center for post-retirement groups could be of immense significance for this purpose. As younger adults need help in establishing communication with their fellows, the older adult comes upon a need to re-establish communication with himself: about who he has been, and who he will decide to be from then on. Toward the end of a busy career, many of us go around talking to ourselves; but this is not quite the same as communicating with ourselves. Without getting too far from family (and physician), the post-retirement individual still needs a place where he can reorder his thoughts in peace, and with some friendly help, in order to redesign his living by some more thoughtful plan.

The residence center for adult study and conference, finally, is not primarily a community-geared agency; but its vitality and growth reflect not its attractiveness as an "escape" from responsibility, but its real power to give nourishment and perspective to people who go there on account of, and on behalf of, their involvement in their adult community and its concerns—whether these be of the intellect, of the arts, or of action.

Rural Life Education

Like little moons, scattered in irregular orbits among the planetary cities, the market centers, lie hundreds of villages; and around and beyond them lies a population for whom "community" means a system of neighboring contacts and kinship relations. The core of this population is the farm family. Its village centers are smaller than 2,500 population. Its contact with the world of influence is by newspaper, radio, and sometimes television. But here too, in most states, the provision of adult learning is promoted by agencies and organizations; only they are not quite the same ones that serve the denizen of the city. Library service is likely to be sparse and hard to reach. The rural school has an integral part to play, of course. But the major agencies are the Co-operative Extension Service of the Department of Agriculture, and the organizations of the farmers themselves.

Here, the grown-up emphasis does not derive from late-come contacts with the community. It derives from the hard struggle to create community among the scattered people; and from a strong and steady reliance on the *family* as the social unit of educational planning.

In many ways, within the Co-operative Extension program, devoted workers, under gifted leadership, have brought farm people into participation in the culture. Cooking and house decoration from grim necessities take on the character of arts, to be enjoyed and understood rather than merely performed. The prevailing philosophy of the Department of Agriculture has for years been that farming is a way of life more than a living; that even if it had to be subsidized, the contribution of the farm family culture to our nation's cultural health is indispensable. Within this philosophy, there has been a steady emphasis in many of the Bureaus on two goals: the development of the individual in his competence and in his confidence in himself as a contributing participant in decision-making and community-building; and the development of the whole-family unit as the life context for the individual. While the rest of our country was following the urban pattern of segregating age groups, sending the 10-year-olds here and inviting the 60-year-olds there, the rural movement was strengthening the older pattern, the events that invited Grandma and the parents and the kids to the same place. Once there, part of the day provided them with their separate activities: the men in a discussion of a soil conservation district, the school-agers in a 4-H meeting, the old people seeing a film or hearing a talk. But for part of the day, the aim was to have business that must be transacted by everyone together, and enjoyments that everyone shared.

The educational standards of the Agricultural Extension program are securely attached in each state to the land-grant college or university through which the Department of Agriculture reaches the local populations. The workers in the field are university employees, trained in problems of rural living. (They are also, of course, responsible to the Department of Agriculture; and, on the county level, to the county authorities as well. This has given a political color to some of their organizational functions, but it is difficult to see how this could have been avoided.) Thus, the largest single adult educational undertaking in the country can be snugly fitted to the widely differing conditions in the various states: to the centralized village organization of the grain states, or to the immense distances between farms in the dry-farming areas of the Great Plains or the range-livestock country.

The standard of achievement which this Service uses for measurement is observed change in farm or household practice. In 1950, it reported well over four million families had changed in the one area, more than three million in the other. As we have no means for evaluating these changes, the record can measure only sheer impact; but it points to another clue to the effectiveness of education, in cases where change *can* be evaluated.

No other adult agency knows more about the interlock among all phases of a culture. While the largest time-segment of county workers, about one third, goes to matters of agricultural production, almost an equal amount of their time goes into areas classified as "rural organization and leadership development; social relationships, adjustments, and cultural values." Even more than agency specialists in cities, these adult education workers must work directly with a wide range of rural organizations: Farm Bureau and Grange or Farmers' Union; schools and college centers; churches; parent groups; civic and service groups; newspapers and radio stations; libraries; women's clubs; state and federal bureaus; chambers of commerce; county government and town officials; and a host of committees, some of which they themselves create. Further, it must not be forgotten that a rapidly growing proportion of America's rural population today is *non*-farm; or that the countryside is being increasingly invaded by "bedroom" subdivisions and commuter estates, whose population brings changes in the needs and the behavior of the county, in its tax resources and its school demands and its governmental pressures.

This rural population is of course served educationally by other means than Agricultural Extension alone.

Homeric efforts by the farm organizations—the Grange, the Farmers' Union, the co-operatives—have shown dividends in study groups, economic and political discussion, bus tours to Washington and to the United Nations, and in local incentives to achievement of many skills, including those of leadership. In the north central regions where farmer-labor partnership has been a tradition, there has been recently an organized effort to train farmer-labor leadership through training conferences under professional sponsorship.

Churches and religious organizations such as the Jewish Agricultural Society, the National Catholic Rural Life Conference, and the Town and Country Committee under the Home Missions Council of the National Council of (Protestant) Churches, all have established programs, or plans for programs, in such areas. The adult educational role of the county public health nurse must not be slighted. Many—though not nearly enough—of our rural counties have county libraries, and state library service is frequently available through schools and organizations. Most of the national welfare and voluntary associations profess an educational intent, and they are not absent from the smallest towns: one Wisconsinite from a town of 160 population deplored the fact that there were so many organizations that nobody had any time to himself any more.

The summary fact about adult learning in rural areas is that because the technology of farming tends to create distance and scattering, the technology of education has had to adapt by taking the teacher to where the people are, rather than bringing the people to where the teacher is. In the most sparsely settled areas of the Great Plains, indeed, Carl Kraenzel has suggested that adult education may have to adopt a fully mobile technology of schoolmobiles and helicopters, supplemented by radio and television.[3] And the learning has also to be pitched very close to the life-needs of production and home economy and family existence. But this has not, in recent practice, prevented significant expansion into areas of world affairs and social questions; it has only helped to ensure that these concerns are dealt with in realistic and grown-up ways. The challenge of rural adult education is one that could invigorate the whole movement, as all of its major agencies converge on meeting it with imagination and energy.

Perhaps the major difference from urban planning, however, is the recognition in rural planning of *regionalism,* in the senses both of recognizing regional differences of social organization based on land use and resources, and of using regional resources in educational programming. This element, stressed by both Loomis and Kraenzel, has been exemplified in the Mountain Plains Area Project, in which a core workshop of leaders from several states spread out into local workshop meetings in their home areas, to develop more concerted thinking about adult education; and in such programs as Per Stensland's regional promotion in West Texas and the American Library Association's "regional library" approach in some southern states. This is a factor which it might be well for the great New York-based national membership organizations to consider more carefully; but we shall come to them in the next chapter.

I have not been concerned, in this unjustly meager résumé, to describe the full scope and practice of these institutions. This has been admirably done in the Fund's studies, and in standard works such as Sheats, Jayne, and Spence. I am more concerned with estimating the direction of movement that they reveal; and my thesis has

[3] Carl F. Kraenzel, *The Great Plains in Transition* (Norman: University of Oklahoma Press, 1955).

been that, on the whole, the movement is toward more fully adult ways of working with adults, on more fully adult levels of interest and need; and that this has tended to come about, or to be reinforced, by involvement with community concerns.

Let me make one distinction clear, on this very point. There is a species of "public relations" policy that agencies have to evolve, which requires them to promote their own interest or membership in other organizations, as school principals belong to Rotary or as librarians push their wares with churches. This aspect of community involvement I should class as politics, rather than as education. When I speak of adult concerns, I mean that people, as people, have certain dreams and desires and needs, and that *organization* is the way they try to realize these. "The community" I speak of is really just the collection, and the context, of such organizations. Organizations exist, first of all, as media through which human beings have to try to reach their goals. This is the *meaning* of any organization to its founders, and to the more perceptive of its members. And it is as educational agencies project themselves into these purposes, make dynamic connection with these meanings, that the agencies themselves acquire status and meaning and importance to the people of the community. They become not joiners but helpers, helpers in the realization of the dreams for which these community organizations stand. As the agencies contribute their skills to the growth of communication among grown people about their intimate concerns, the agencies in their turn grow up, and become serviceable to the adult community. This is the consensus of their experience; and this is, I hope, the direction of their destiny.

CHAPTER 5 *Discusses Associations and Councils*

In no country in the world has the principle of association been more successfully used or applied to a greater multitude of objects than in America. . . . Americans of all ages, all conditions, and all dispositions constantly form associations . . . to give entertainments, to found seminaries, to build inns, to construct churches, to diffuse books, to send missionaries to the antipodes. . . . If it is proposed to inculcate some truth or to foster some feeling by the encouragement of a great example, they form a society.

—Alexis de Tocqueville,
Democracy in America

W HAT ARE loosely called the voluntary organizations are as diverse as the ends for which people associate together. More than ten dozen formally organized nationwide associations are members of a body known as the Council of National Organizations, which in turn is an organ of the Adult Education Association of the U.S.A. The published report of their educational functions is admirably classified and tabulated under a wealth of varying factors of similarity and difference; but even this does not exhaust their infinite variety. Within the limits of this present book, however, we are concerned only with those organizations that try to provide a structure and content for study by local groups, and those that try to involve their members in the shaping of opinion and attitude on certain matters of public concern, through educational means such as conferences and workshops. The sorts of organization I am excluding are exemplified by professional societies that work chiefly through committees seeking to advance the interests of the membership, and resource agencies chiefly providing pamphlet materials or press-radio releases for general consumption.

For the individual in his own home town, these national bodies are visible in the shape of local clubs. Wherever we wandered, in the grand tour of 1955, such clubs were in impressive evidence. In few places did we fail to find a League of Women Voters, a College Women's Club, a service club, units of national religious organizations; and of course a host of local clubs not affiliated with any national. We met members of farm organizations, of co-ops, of Homemakers Clubs, of Junior Leagues, and of the omnipresent P.T.A.

Viewed at the national level, these direct-service membership associations present an impressive picture. Thirty-three of them report employing over five thousand professional workers, and nearly six thousand office workers. The function of staff, as we all know, is to guide the membership and train the board in making policy, and then to carry out the policies they have helped make. In addition, most of the national staffs prepare materials, study kits, discussion guides, and bibliographies, and plan for conferences and workshops and institutes for members or staff on various levels, from national to local. Their stated educational aims are strictly sterling: to help their members work for community and world improvement; to influence action on legislation and public policies in such fields as education, health, economics, good government; to work toward wholeness in community living; to improve the ability of adults to form sound and independent judgments on questions of public policy; to train members to co-operate in the preservation of values significant in home life; to provide individual guidance for the individual pursuing self-education; and so on and on.

Among the most important goals stated, and worked for, by many of these organizations—particularly women's —is the enlistment and training of members for volunteer service in their communities. This is a dimension too frequently overlooked in adult learning: helping the individual to *use* himself in guided and thoughtful ways. The uses offered range from welfare service to legislative lobbying, with an important share going to work in the interracial and interfaith fields.

Methods approved by these associations, and inculcated through leader-training and promotional conferences, range from speaker-and-questions to intensive focused study groups. The decisions as to policy and program are usually made "at National," which is likely to mean somewhere on upper Broadway in New York City. But New York is a highly specialized and eccentric culture, which attracts professionals with the missionary impulse. It is the layman's Home Missions center; and its mission is to show the rest of us how we can better achieve our goals. Except for a few national organizations housed in the free-floating, somewhat alienated metropolis of the District of Columbia (where they can keep an eye on the Congress), and one or two pioneers that have homed in on Chicago, the bulk of the clubs to which we all belong have their treasuries, their Home Offices, and their policy-making powers immured in that most but least American of cities, Manhattan. Dexter Keezer has even questioned whether New York "Nationals" have any "locals." This is an understandable hyperbole; but it does point to a question of import for adult learning—that of the relationship of the National and the local.

Basically, the "National" exists because it recognizes needs and strivings among adults in all our cities and towns, and because it has in mind ways in which those strivings can be made more effective. State organizations, usually grouped into geographical assemblies that are not quite truly regional in operation, are supported in the job of keeping local groups active. And it is the local groups, finally, that reach the living individuals who seek to realize one or another of their aims by identifying them with those of the organization. Here is the real scene of action. Here are the clubs.

At the local level, luck is a large factor in the effectiveness of these voluntary clubs. One year's strong leader makes one town's strong program; the same club in another town or another year may be negligible in its educational effort.

A serious detriment to the effectiveness of individual clubs is usually the multiple duplications of membership. The average active woman who is a member of one is probably a member of at least three. In a California county where I worked some years ago, the two strongest clubs were the University Women and the Parent-Teachers Association. The issue before the county was whether to establish a county library system to replace the old practice of distributing adult books through the rural schools. The P.T.A. voted to take as its year's project the defeating of that plan. The AAUW voted to take as its the promotion of that plan. Nothing surprising in this, of course. What surprised me was to find that a majority of the board members of the two clubs were *the same women,* using, as I have written elsewhere, "their Tuesday membership to vote against their Monday purposes."

Even in less extreme cases, multiple belonging tends to lessen the individual's effort in any one role—even though

our familiar experience is that "only the busiest people
can find time to take on more jobs." It is the Nationals'
job to *upgrade* local program and leadership. But with
fifty national staffs working at this job, the results filter
down to individuals, only part of whose attention can be
given to any one program. Abundant testimony suggests
that the really effective upgrading, in leadership, in volunteer development, in program and methods effectiveness,
has come most often from local and nearby sources of professional help: university or college, or an adult agency
with professional staff and experience. The other major
local resource is the occasionally successful co-ordination
or pooling that can happen among particular organizations, or even better through some form of active council
that includes professional resources.

One outstanding example of university-sponsored local
co-ordination that I visited was the State Organization
Service (S.O.S.) of the University of Minnesota's General
Extension Division. Here, in one headquarters building, is
a comprehensive facility open to all educational bodies
in the state. To its then thirty-seven member organizations
it offered office space, clerical service, accounting and
fund-custody service, program counseling, conference and
meeting arrangement, and assistance in running the organization. It maintained addressograph and other equipment
too expensive for many of the members to maintain for
themselves. It had university financial support, and also
received fees for services performed for its members. It
housed a book and pamphlet center which could stock any
member's materials, for gift or sale.

Among the members are not only single associations,
such as the League of Women Voters and United World
Federalists, but also a number of firmly co-ordinated bodies
such as the Minnesota Council on Adult Education, whose
nearly one hundred member agencies include institutions,
government agencies, private associations, and educational

groups—including again the League and the UWF. Another co-ordinating body with a fine record of achievement is the Minnesota World Affairs Center, a federation of twenty-three organizations—many of them also members of the Council and of the S.O.S. This Center is itself housed in the S.O.S., and is itself a member of the Adult Education Council. It gives program and materials service to all the world-affairs groups which comprise it; and sometimes puts on its own programs, or sponsors events in behalf of its whole membership. In 1954–55 the Center collaborated with the Minneapolis *Star* in putting out a series of newspaper tabloid "Guides to the Study of World Affairs," which were used in schools and by adult groups throughout the Twin Cities. Several locals of national associations, thus, hold multiple memberships in interlocking Centers and Councils within their own locality.

Another notable example of local co-ordination is the Adult Education Council of Denver, long famous and still strong. This institution, expertly but meagerly staffed, and housed in the public library, performs a number of services for its members, and also initiates multi-organizational projects in international affairs, in leadership training, in program planning, and in various subject fields of general interest. Working closely with the library and with the Community College of the University of Denver, the Council is able to maintain the high program standards among the city's many organizations which their related Nationals would like to maintain but cannot, by themselves and at their distance.

Chattanooga has recently developed a similar Council, which I shall come back to describe in a later chapter. The Memphis Adult Education Council was sponsoring thirty-nine discussion groups of its own in 1955. The New York Adult Education Council, under the veteran guidance of Winifred Fisher, has adventured along these and other lines, such as adult counseling and the promotion of additional public adult learning facilities.

The strong suggestion from these strong local centers is that the local affiliate of the national association gains most of its strength from local resources, and from collaboration with its local neighbors. The single body finds itself linked to several co-ordinating bodies or centers, and still maintains its own identity and its tie with the National.

On the whole, the local, state, and regional Adult Education Council has not realized the promise which it once seemed to have. Twenty-five such councils are listed in the 1948 edition of Mary Ely's *Handbook of Adult Education.* In 1955, twenty of them were still in business, within a total of fifty-six councils and associations: twenty-two local, thirty state, and four regional. The Adult Education Association from year to year proposes plans for increasing and strengthening the association within states and cities of the people who work with adults in the task of learning. But progress is slow, in part because not enough workers in the adult vineyard identify themselves with the adult education movement; in part because they are busy with their own programs, and meet each other at enough professional conferences without adding one more; and in large part because associations and councils require money, which is hard to come by.

The real focus of adult learning, however, despite all the New York, Washington, or Chicago head offices, is still on the local level. I want to return to this topic a little later; but first let's look at two other forms of association which have undertaken educational responsibilities: Industry, and the Church.

Labor and Industry

Just as a whole field of learning has grown up around production from the soil, and rural living, and co-operative organization, so another has grown up around the urban industrial focus. What is familiar as "workers' education" is, in our country, only one facet of a total push that includes learning for the job, in shop or in management, and learning for organization, whether union or front-office. And now, both sets of learnings have burst the bounds of local interest and are beginning to face the world that conditions their existence. Significant break-through points are becoming visible, and these too have much promise of interest to the rest of the educational movement.

The transition, in Ernest Schwartztrauber's phrase, from industrial warfare to industrial government, and the great leap of union membership from some three million to a good sixteen million in twenty years, has placed enormous responsibility upon both union and industrial leaders. The early days of Sam Gompers reading Marx aloud to his fellow cigar-wrappers, or of the young immigrants and southern mill workers whose hunger for schooling was so eloquently described by Hilda Smith, are past. Free public schooling, to whose establishment the labor movement contributed beyond measure in the early nineteenth century, removed from American workers the need to find substitutes for schooling, the need that motivated much of the early greatness of the Workers' Education movement in Britain. So when labor's cause was a militant cause, up to some twenty years ago, its education laid stress on the study of the labor movement and its social and political promise. As unionism became the standard and millions of new members poured in, not always of their own choice, the learning emphasis had to turn more and more toward union skills: how to run a meeting, how to negotiate, how to be a shop steward. Even at the Labor Education Workshops I attended in the summer of 1955, the paramount questions which the educational representatives brought were how to get people to come to meetings, and how to keep them from leaving.

The result has been that most courses have been for union

management—officers and staff—rather than for membership at large. The Ladies Garment Workers Union, for
example, has reached perhaps the pinnacle of educational
influence in making certification by its Education Department a prerequisite to union office, and in creating a full-
time year's program of education leading to a guarantee
of officership or staff employment. University courses for
labor men, at such places as Harvard, Chicago, and perhaps a score of others, have stressed "human relations" in
union management and representation in negotiations.
Many of their students, incidentally, graduated from a
union course into a management position.

Meantime, however, the efforts of university and other
professional planners for labor education (for example, at
the Wisconsin Summer School for Workers, one of the
oldest university efforts in this field) have been steadily to
recruit general union membership by arranging courses
of more general interest. The most consistent job in this
direction has been done by the many-purposed American
Labor Education Service, which has worked through union
management into union membership, ultimately involving
several thousands in programs on the United Nations and
on international affairs, in a variety of areas from New
York to Minneapolis and Detroit and the Plains states. The
national labor bodies and several of their member Inter-
nationals have given strong support to this broad attack;
and religious bodies, like the Jewish Labor Committee,
the National Conference of Churches, and Catholic labor
organs have tried to introduce social awareness as an educational goal.

As with other national membership associations, the
work of planning and preparing materials for union study
is done mostly at the national level; and there is the usual
gradient, if not gap, between national plans and local
execution. In view of this fact, the words of Mark Starr,
educational director of the ILGWU and author of the

Fund's Labor Education report, gain added power: the essential problem, says Starr, is "how to develop, out of this awareness of confused and tragic events, an understanding of complex issues, a sense of human brotherhood and world community"; but on the local scene, where workers live and breathe and have their being, "workers' education has thus far not integrated the activity of the unions into the life of the community." In short, as with other national membership associations, strong and wise leadership from the top is not always enough to ensure educational success at local levels. Here again, the greatest local successes are likely to involve *joint* effort with local institutions: collaboration between union and library, union and university, union and World Affairs Council, or the like.

Another way to reach the worker with educational programs is on the job, in the plant. The obvious uses for this method are to retrain workers for the introduction of new methods, or new company policies. But its potential is somewhat more significant than just this. And here is another point at which the best leadership is thinking beyond present practices. The basic incentive is of course to increase productivity; but there are two other factors involved. First, while the effects on employment of the drive toward automation are still moot, most employers can foresee a situation in which the work load is decreasing, but in which they are still unwilling to reduce the work week. At many points in industry there is actually time for training meetings; and there may be more elbowroom still to come. Second, according to Albert Nickerson of the Socony-Vacuum Oil Company, "A survey of seventy-six American corporations revealed that lack of specific skills accounted for only a shade over 10 per cent of discharges, while character traits accounted for virtually 90 per cent." Similarly with promotions: "While a man's technical knowledge may be his best tool during his first five years or so with our company, in many cases this curve tends to flatten out on the value chart and is met by the ascendant curve of the man's skill in human relations."[1]

It is this phase, *human relations*, that emblazons the largest of the several banners carried by the advancing forces of education within industry. Pioneered by Harvard Business School, by Cornell and Penn State, I found it the substance of an ambitious program developed by Ohio University for the Pennsylvania Railroad. One man from Ohio and one from Penn State traveled the length of the Pennsylvania system for months, talking with employees at all levels and gathering case material on their problems—on the road, in the plant, at home. Translated into cases a little farther removed from personal experience, these materials were then organized into a case-study syllabus which was used, in open-ended free discussion courses of several weeks, with top management and with succeeding echelons down to gang foremen on the road. In California, I met a group of training directors who had had a ten-week workshop with a group dynamics expert from the University on "Human Relations Training." Along with this emphasis, I met others: courses for employees in economics, ranging from frank management apologetics to open discussion of the problems of a competitive economy made up of closely controlled elements. I myself set up groups in economics which were attended by supervisors and junior management men from several industries. I talked with an official of the Baltimore and Ohio Railroad who was seeking a way of enlisting the employees in genuinely participative discussions of company policies. I heard of "joint time" courses that met in plants from four to six, with the company contributing one hour and the men one. I noted the growing number of universities that are contributing to this trend, and the growing number of companies that have decided it is better to do it themselves than to have uni-

[1] Albert Nickerson, "Climbing the Managerial Ladder," *Saturday Review*, November 21, 1953.

versities come in and do it for them. But nowhere did I
find any strong opposition to the trend itself; and I am
holding my breath waiting to see if there may develop here
a real break-through into a new opportunity for learning,
a new kind of school for workers.

Significantly, the greatest difficulties in this area are reported from efforts to use in-plant human-relations groups
to help union stewards and shop foremen understand each
other better. At present, the decision seems to be to deal
with the two groups separately; here, the conflict of loyalties is too acute to overcome with methods still in their
untried infancy. But the same trouble appeared on the level
of university services in Industrial Relations: in general,
the faculties reported better success in dealing with first
one camp and then the other, with only a few men, like
Phillips Garman of Illinois, able to handle both together.

In-plant education is a field for which no teachers are
prepared. Training directors are sought from all walks of
life, with the prayer that professional guidance can be
found for them later. The emphasis on "human relations" is
wishful rather than expert, so far: in the words of Father
Andrew Boss, to a conference of the Western Regional Division of the National Association of Training Directors,
"Once the conferees left the area of technical training and
moved into the realm of human relations, confusion of
thought and words sucked them into marshy ground and
they went under blowing bubbles with their last words as
they sank out of sight." But the impulse that is embodied
in that phrase may be the forerunner to what management
now calls "the need for liberal education": an attempt to
introduce educational occasions for the purpose of developing intelligence. Either it *is* that, or it is a phony.

Management

One of the most interesting developments in recent years
has been the growth of this demand for "liberal education

for Management." A section of *The Saturday Review of Literature* was devoted to it in the fall of 1953; two leading articles dealt with it in *The Harvard Business Review* in 1954; *Harper's* in March, 1955, carried the story of Bell Telephone's experiment in sending several of its second-echelon executives back to college for liberal arts training. Universities are establishing "Executive Development" workshops; and the American Management Association has developed a literature on the subject.

The education of management begins with the bread-and-butter subjects, just as union training does. The new element is an emphasis on the humanities, and on a broad approach to the problems of modern civilization. While university training for business careers began seventy-five years ago, with the Wharton School, and increased greatly within the last thirty, more or less formal plans of management development in most larger industries began within the last five. No two industries use the same approach or report the same philosophy; but the reports on Management Education by the American Management Association seem to converge around certain common issues: Who should do the training, where should it be done, how should it be related to recruitment? A strong recommendation in the summary report finds the industries actually recruiting an "officer class" from the universities, without admitting that in doing so they are violating the tradition of truly equal opportunity for all potential leaders; and argues that the industries themselves should provide the university training for non-college men of ability, while they are with the firm. "It must be realized . . . that the intellectual development of future business leaders cannot be dealt with effectively if it is treated as two separate agencies, educational institutions and business corporations, at two separate stages in the life of the individual. It must be treated as a single process applied in each instance to a single individual, the future high executive, and it should be continuous throughout each individual's active life." [2]

The emphasis, also, is on *general* education. The report cites, with approval, a passage from *General Education in a Free Society*: "In this epoch in which almost all of us must be experts in some field in order to make a living, general education therefore assumes a peculiar importance. . . . The aim of general education may be defined as that of providing the broad critical sense by which to recognize competence in any field. William James said that an educated man knows a good man when he sees one." [3] With this Aristotelian notion goes the further idea, born of experience, that a good technical man does not automatically make a good president: he knows how to make decisions in his field, but may lack the comprehension of what those decisions mean to the broad American economy.

Further, the report maintains that there is a close connection between "an effective program of management development" and "the general philosophy of a corporation toward the education of *all* its employees." Such philosophies at present range from none to such statements as, "Management's responsibility to employee education should be to do all it thinks needs to be done to provide employees with whatever is necessary to become better citizens"; or, "To make the education program ring true, the worker, on his job, must experience a free society for eight hours a day." [4]

The social roots of this new urgency would be of interest for speculation. A practical one is suggested by Mr. Nickerson: "Contrary to the notion that many people have, business does not become more centralized as it becomes larger and more complex, nor do its employees become

[2] L. F. Urwick, *Management Education in American Business* (New York: American Management Association, 1954), pp. 49–50.
[3] *Ibid.*, p. 51.
[4] *Ibid.*, pp. 51–52.

subservient to a comparatively small number of powerful
men. Exactly the opposite situation prevails. As our industrial society becomes more mature and more productive it
tends to decentralize steadily and to require increasing
numbers of educated and able men." [5] A historical one is
suggested by Lt. Col. Urwick, who wrote the summary report in the AMA series (italics are mine): "Two allied
tendencies which had already been in evidence since 1910
accelerated sharply. The first of these was *the divorce of
ownership from management*; increasingly the larger corporations were conducted by men who had little or no stake
in them as stockholders. The second was the growing recognition that management . . . was a discrete skill, *a profession in itself* calling for both theoretical and practical
training." [6]

A further important clue lies in the developing role of
management men *outside* of industry. As the Roosevelt administration brought the professions into government, so
the Eisenhower administration brought in Management.
And in our cities, the "public service" role of managerial
personnel has grown steadily. In my own city, for example, the part of the iceberg of power that shows above the
surface comprises perhaps a hundred men who among them
manage the organizational life of the town. They hold the
agency board memberships, run the campaigns, manage
the Co-ordinating Council and Council of Social Agencies
and Community Chest, the Association and the Junior Association of Commerce; they buy the ball teams and hold
the power of consent over parks and schools and housing
and Right Opinion generally. In their business capacity,
they are mostly upper-echelon executives. In their public
service capacity, they constitute the "management" of the
community. Below them range several echelons of juniors,
who are annually tested as fund-drive section chairmen,

[5] Nickerson, *op. cit.*
[6] Urwick, *op. cit.*, p. 24.

committeemen, and so on. The top group is acutely conscious of its own problems of over-involvement and of self-replacement. Its spokesmen show an awareness of the need for broadly experienced and broadly educated leaders that is parallel to the growing awareness of the same need in industry as a whole.

While I would not assert the full thesis of the "managerial revolution," my own hunch is that events have thrust upon this class of men increasing measures of responsibility, during their own lifetime; and they are uncertain of their succession because their class is the first to face the problem, because it has too lately come to power. Feeling some sense that they are installed now as the most-favored class, and likely to remain so, they feel an uneasy responsibility for becoming educated up to their station. I suspect that it is this feeling, too, which has generated their attitude of *noblesse oblige*, suggested by the proposal for "continuing education" all down the ranks.

The Fund for Adult Education, I think, showed real perspicuity in including them among major resources for adult learning. The challenge that faces adult education is to evaluate and integrate this new force into the long-familiar resource structure, to find what its potential is and how it may best be encouraged to serve the general movement.

Churches

A special category of local institution within a national membership organization is the churches. They differ from the rest mainly because of the role assigned to "the Church" within our culture. But when they essay adult education programs, their functions and successes are open to the same set of judgments that we apply to other institutions.

Unhappily, there is insufficient data at hand on this set of activities. Knowles estimated fifteen and a half million adults as the educational clientele of religious institutions.

This included all those in adult church schools. Seventeen national religiously oriented or sponsored associations are listed in the Council of National Organizations; these do not include the YMHA or YWHA. In addition, we have already noted national religious agencies, Catholic, Jewish, and Protestant, for service to workers and farmers. Nevertheless, I should hesitate to grant that more than a third of all active learning occasions in this country were the work of the churches.

The basic ambivalence in church adult education is parallel to that in labor-union education. The goal that justifies the effort is, to the church, the making of, say, better Baptists; to the community, it is the making of better citizens. The semantic meeting ground is likely to be on some such phrase as "better Christians," which ideally would satisfy both. Or, as one national religious organization puts it, "In its adult education program the organization stresses increased knowledge of the truths of religion and advancement in personal holiness" through "religious discussion clubs which aim at having participants make a significant contribution to Christian living in the community."

Much of the effort of church organizations on the national or regional scale is on more familiar and mundane grounds: teacher training for church classes, leader training for adult groups, conference and institute leadership for working with problems of the organization itself. Other educational efforts are directed to the reduction of bias and prejudice, by means of sponsored publications and encouragement to discussion groups and community service programs. Directed volunteer service, such as that sponsored by the American Friends Service Committee, or by local congregations interested in housing or rehabilitation, is again a useful kind of adult education. But where shall we classify courses in biblical scholarship, in Jewish history and literature, in fundamentalist dogma, in Christian Science, in Buddhism? And is a course on anthropology or modern art to be classed with religious education if it is given by a church?

Like other national membership organizations, the church is most easily visible as a local entity with a building, a pastor, a congregation, and a deficit. Membership identity, however, differs from that of lay associations in the feeling of kinship with a sort of universal congregation: the assertion "I am a Methodist" is not equivalent to "I am a member of Rotary." Without exploring the fascinating implications of this remark, let's merely say that member loyalty is presumably stronger in attachment to a church than to most lay associations. Yet most churches lament the apathy of their members, the sparsity of attendance at their educational meetings, just as the rest of us do.

As with other membership societies, the national organization supplies certain incentives, directions, and materials, but local program strength is a function of local resources and leadership. The national programs grow naturally out of the respective religions: the Catholic tending to emphasize the application of Catholic doctrine to current problems; the Jewish tending to emphasize action for the advancement of tolerance and the welfare and charitable activities that are so strong a part of the Jewish tradition; the Protestant projecting activity programs chiefly on the basis of "the social Gospel" and the translation of Christianity into the pursuit of humane values in community life. There is also, of course, some specialization along doctrinal lines.

The local church or synagogue, however, tends to build its adult activity program out of the interests of its leader and its congregation. A church in Los Angeles twenty years ago opened a "College of Life" that in two years had an enrollment of thirty-four hundred adults from the whole surrounding area, in courses on family relations, dramatic production, poetry, folk dancing, psychology, bridge.

A. Powell Davies' Unitarian Church in Washington, D.C., maintains an adult education department with its own annex and a broad range of interests. Wilbur Hallenbeck studied ten New York churches and found that only 10 per cent of their adult activity offerings were in the field of religious education *per se*.

In this kind of program, the church becomes just another private adult education agency. But being "the Church," with a feeling of responsibility for all ages and across the whole of living, its tendency would normally be to feel that it should develop some sort of total program, and that "unless it is leading the community, its doors will close." This tendency is supported by the argument, stated for example by Bernard Meland in *The Church and Adult Education*, that "there are problems growing out of the church and state relationship, the rural and urban conflict, capitalism and labor, and racial justice, which . . . church people will be compelled to confront, . . . but which they will be incapable of facing intelligently unless some effort is made to enlighten them upon these issues."

The assumption here is that if these people are to take stands on these issues *as church people*, only the church can supply the appropriate enlightenment. But, like other agencies of enlightenment, the church sometimes forgets how many other identities these people have. They must confront these same issues as workers: therefore the union should enlighten them. Or as citizens: therefore a host of civic education associations will do it. And so will press, radio, and television; and their friends.

Within the local community, in short, enlightenment is a competitive industry. The force of any one program upon the individual will be the resultant of two variables: his degree of identification with, or "loyalty" to, the sponsoring institution; and the inherent excellence of the program itself, viewed by objective standards of effectiveness.

Educational Television

At several points I have mentioned the use of television, and a word should be said here about the current potentials of educational television. It seems reasonable to discuss it here since there is a National Association that guides the destinies of these stations; and of local councils that are trying to create additional stations. But actually ETV is an unknown in the woodpile.

It is beyond question that television will bring unguessed revolution into our political life, and can be more powerful than radio in creating a mass acceptance for information and culture that would not have been reached for by most people if it had not reached out for them. The overwhelming popularity of Professor Baxter's Shakespeare programs on the West Coast matches (within the proportional limits of ETV) the enormous audiences created by commercial productions of Shakespeare's plays: more people were said to have seen *Richard III* on a Sunday in March, 1956, than had seen it in all of its stage presentations since it was written.

The Fund for Adult Education maintains a Center where television program films are distributed for educational use. They are being used; they are also being criticized for being too "schoolmasterish," with much talk and little dynamic visualization. The educator, here, feels an acute inferiority before the challenge of professional presentation in this medium. The ETV Committee in my own city was offered eighteen half-hours on commercial TV channels, and decided not to accept them because its advisers said there were not enough professional resources available to ensure good programs.

A serious problem is that most ETV stations have been assigned ultra-high-frequency channels, and that the cost of converting ordinary receiving sets to UHF is just enough to deter most people from converting. Therefore, the most successful ETV stations have been those assigned standard VHF channels, such as Channel 9 in San Francisco or Channel 11 in Chicago. In the face of this obstacle, several ETV committees, like Baltimore's, have withdrawn from the attempt to compete; and some stations that had already gone "on the air" have gone off again.

In the meantime, several programs on commercial television have accomplished stupendous successes: in that same month of March, 1956, Edward Murrow brought the heads of state of two nations in critical conflict into face-to-face communication with more Americans, probably, than there are people in either of those nations. Our own domestic political conventions and campaigns are in for some revolutionary changes since public men and public issues have become, at last, truly visible.

The broadcast transmission of instruction has already begun, and holds the promise of making our more exciting and persuasive teachers available to more millions than they could ever before have contemplated. If this moves ahead, it may bring in its train more emphasis on the use of other teachers in a discussion-leader capacity. It may, if not challenged in time, merely create more incentive for passive learning, which is no learning. As used in cities like Portland, where TV panels on issues in international affairs are preceded by distribution of fact-sheets and followed by home or club listener-discussion groups and newspaper ballot forms, it could lead to an unguessable increase in public communication and in the stimulation of open inquiry into all manner of questions.

My honest opinion at this time is that we have no means of predicting the scope of the revolution that television education may trigger off; but the chances are that the commercial innovators will have got the major share of such revolutions under way, through programs that tax us through the prices of advertised commodities, before Educational Television has raised enough volunteer dollars to take over the command of this technological revolution in learning.

Private Agencies

Another segment of educational effort not touched by the Fund's reports is that of the independent private agencies. These have been of tremendous importance in the development of methods, materials, and philosophies of adult learning, and in developing program for particular sections within the community; or programs in special fields of subject interest, like health or world affairs. Their sources have been largely the personal inspiration of one or a few people; their function, to pioneer in ways that the public agencies could not—just as, once, the private nursery schools pioneered a whole philosophy and practice of primary teaching. The nursery school and kindergarten, however, were eventually accepted into the public system. The pioneering adult agencies have seldom—well, whichever it is: been accepted, or succumbed.

To take a single example, the Boston Center for Adult Education has operated since 1933 with a fee program of informal group studies in all types of subject: language, arts, dramatics, foreign affairs, crafts, and almost any desired subject. From the beginning it made use of knowledgeable laymen as group leaders, giving them staff help in learning how to succeed with adult groups. Its aims are simply stated: "To meet a special need for a place where mature men and women can develop their latent powers, in congenial surroundings, without thought of certificates and diplomas."

The Boston Center illustrates another unique function of the informal private agency: the ability to persuade adults that they *can* learn without "feeling silly" about "going back to school." This fear I encountered again in reports in other cities. In Louisville, the branch library

learning programs are a boon to many who don't want to
be seen going into the main library, for fear people would
think them ignorant—or that the librarians would find them
so. (The "many" here include an evening high school principal.) In Denver, an adult counselor at Denver University
said her biggest task was to get people over the fear of
somehow losing their adult standing by "going back" to
classes. The small private agency, by making its invitation
informal and tailoring it to particular small populations,
has done more than is realized to awaken in our people
the courage to learn again.

But the small agency, with all its virtues, is the sport of
chance and personality; and while it belongs to the local
Council, it still pursues its own way without being very
much concerned with the whole community picture. It
can't do the whole job; no one can; so who can take responsibility for worrying about it?

Community Organization

"There have always been, in any given community, certain obvious weaknesses in this division of responsibility,"
wrote Glen Burch in 1948. "These weaknesses, which have
become more and more apparent as the movement has
grown in scope, have stemmed, first, from the fact that the
division of responsibility among a variety of adult education agencies has never . . . been co-operatively planned,
and, second, from the fact that since, for most organizations, adult education activities have been marginal to a
larger program . . . they have tended to serve the institutional ends of the sponsoring agency rather than the needs
of the people of the community. . . . The problem of
community organization for adult education is not simply
a matter of developing . . . a single program calculated to
meet the continuing educational needs of its adult population. It is rather one of assuring maximum co-operation

. . . of securing an optimum balancing of a given community's educational resources."[7]

The real job of "enlightenment" remains local and personal. It is that of integrating the citizen himself around goals, values, and action-patterns which the piecemeal efforts of his many guides will contribute to, rather than confuse. And this requires more genuine efforts to make the patterns of enlightenment by community agencies hang together in a more coherent pattern, to work together for the creation of an active adult community culture. In the good words of Howard McClusky, long a student and a mover in community integration, "It seems that as far as possible the whole front of community interest must be promoted and cultivated if specific projects and separate aspects are to be advanced."

I myself have never seen—and have long been asking—why we could not develop a kind of thinking in which the whole city was seen as the campus of adult learning: its industries, its libraries, its churches, its schools, its clubs and agencies. Indeed, I once frightened the entire American Association for Adult Education (this was back in 1939) by suggesting that the adult educators should speak in behalf of the whole community, as an interest superior to their disparate ones, and with the intent of *orchestrating* adult learning into a symphonic whole.

This remains a dream, and to many people a sort of nightmare of collectivism. But it is only the other side of the essential coin of adult learning: the integration of the individual around his own purposes and those he shares with other men. We are fractioned and dispersed among our many roles and aims; and education is our search for wholeness.

Why, then, is wholeness so difficult to attain? Why, after

[7] Glen Burch, "Community Organization for Adult Education," in *Handbook of Adult Education*, Mary Ely, ed. (New York: Institute of Adult Education, 1948), p. 281.

a generation's efforts at community integration in adult education alone, are we so far from reaching it?

Some believe that our inherent respect for the privacy of the diverse goals of diverse individuals compels us to a policy of laissez-faire, just as we respect the right of churches or hospitals to attract their own clients. This is true, as regards private learning goals. But I am speaking here of the concert of efforts to help people reach common goals, primary among these being communication with one another about their important common aims. The fact that our hospitals often are not very well organized, and our religious sects not quite in free communion with each other, has no bearing on the need to create the fullest measure of intellectual communication within the province of learning which is in the service of adult purposes.

Second, it has been asserted that the ego-needs of existing organizations keep interagency councils impotent to make real decisions of emphasis and policy that might affect any given agency. This too is true. Most councils, unless they have unusual leadership, serve not as a community board of strategy but as a place where the agencies can keep a watchful eye on each other, and keep alert to what others are up to. Few councils would dare to advise a member agency about its own internal program, or to suggest the actual elimination of wasteful or competitive duplications. There is frequent consultation between two agencies that might help each other; but there is no collective voice able to shape a city's program as a whole.

Organizations do tend to perpetuate themselves, and to argue their inherent sovereignty. Also, aims and methods do differ as among different nationally identified groups, some stressing political action, some the comparison of ideas about what action to take, and so on. Here again, the problem is not exclusive to education. What are called health organizations, but are really special-illness-defense groups like heart, cancer, polio, and the like, in most cities are unable to coalesce into a common council or to wage common campaigns. Largely, this is because of their proprietary interest each in some one disease; I have believed that if they met on the common ground of promoting health, instead of fighting disease, they could get together. And so with our agencies of adult learning: the combat against special fields of ignorance makes us proprietary; but our common business is communication, and this I believe can, as it should, begin at home.

A more serious aspect of this last problem is the inherent tendency of every major agency that *could* become the leader and center of a community's search for knowledge to feel that it *should* become so; and hence to come into competitive rather than supportive relation to its colleagues in other agencies. In a good-sized western city, some fifty miles from the State University, there are adult programs sponsored by the Junior College, the Evening High School, and a State College. To one of their directors, I said, "Do you fellows work closely together?"

"You bet we do," he said; "we watch each other like dogs."

"But isn't there something you all collaborate on together?"

"Sure there is. We all work together to keep the Extension Division out of here."

In the graphs of present and wished-for school programming, there was something like a 50 per cent increase projected in school leadership in the community and in school use of non-school facilities; and the self-study committees urged that "*the schools* take a position of leadership in the city." We have seen Meland citing the same desire on the part of the churches; and we need no citations to remind us of how many other agencies believe they could assume that somewhat mythical "leadership."

Yet, against the evidence that leads to the easy assumption that collaboration is impossible, more and more examples do exist to show that real teamwork does occur—under certain conditions. Among those conditions are the recognition that no agency can do it alone; the working out of a structural articulation of the parts of one job distributed among various partners; and the existence of professional leadership and resources at the core of that particular program.

The third major obstacle that is asserted to stand in the way of community organization for adult learning is one that comes from outside the movement itself. It is what it has become stylish to call "the power structure" of the community. I myself once wrote of San Francisco: "Even though most of the money for charitable and cultural institutions comes from the anonymous multitudes in the middle brackets, the influence of the name-bearing families is decisive in the making of policy for those enterprises. And even though there is no conscious policy maintained by the influential group, by distributing its interests between the arts and education, between left-wing and right-wing programs, it manages to keep its control effective over everything that comes into its general sphere of interest. The liberal arts, including those of liberal thought, are continuously maintained, so that if one agency disappears another rises to take its place; but the stream of liberal activity in the patronage-supported agencies never rises above a certain level in proportion to the total life of the city. And no considerable challenge to the ruling culture or control has ever come from institutions which it supported." [8]

Saul Alinsky, in a recent conversation, put it another way. The essence of free education, he said, is inquiry; and inquiry comes ever closer to the sources of authority.

[8] John Walker Powell, *School for Americans* (New York: American Association for Adult Education, 1942).

At some point, the process of inquiry begins to threaten even the authority that sponsored it; and so must stop. And therefore the educational goal of unhindered free inquiry can never be attained.

These are both hypotheses, with some support in experience. Their suggestion is that any attempt at fully concerted efforts to advance adult learning in all important lines would find obstacles put in its path. This, however, we shall not know until it has been tried. Where it has been approached, the "power structure" has itself been part of the planning and operating structure. The recent incursion of high-echelon industrial management into the ranks of those who promote, and take part in, adult learning processes has introduced a factor whose weight cannot be predicted. Management is beginning to believe that only educated men can handle its level of responsibility. If it begins to appear that only educated cities can handle the responsibilities of civilization in this half of the twentieth century, I believe that educated cities will be achieved. I assert now my belief that this is so; and I shall discuss later the conditions that seem to be required for moving in the necessary direction. For the present point, however, the moral is simply this: that none of the asserted obstacles to integrating a community's educational efforts is finally proved, none is really unassailable. Our efforts toward educational concert have shown some progress. It is reasonably clear that the true strength of organization for adult learning rests on local integration. But it is also quite clear that we have not yet found the key that will open that door, and keep it open, to its full width.

CHAPTER 6 *Denies that the Present Patterns Are Adequate*

> Looking closely at the practice [of adult education], one has a strong feeling that this collection of trees simply does not naturally make a wood.
>
> —C. Hartley Grattan,
> *In Quest of Knowledge*

ADULT EDUCATION is everybody's job, and nobody's business: this is the conclusion to which I am driven by our summary review of agencies and associations.

Somehow, with the hundreds of organizations and institutions serving millions of adults, *the real job of education for maturity is not getting done, and cannot be done in this fashion.*

I am not thinking of the quantitative incompleteness of these programs; though too many towns and counties are without libraries, too many cities without full-time adult educational personnel, too many states without anything resembling adequate University Extension service, too many organizations without adequate standards of planning and leadership, and too many adult citizens without access or incentive to learning.

The problem arises from other factors, for which the agencies and institutions are not to blame. It is not their

90

fault, but simply inherent in their history and their situation, that they are inadequate at present for the task that waits doing. The factors in their inadequacy are common to them all; and they must be faced as sober fact.

First: *Every one of them was created, and still exists, for a primary purpose other than the education of adults.*

The basic job of Agricultural Extension is, after all, vocational agriculture and household economics; the provision for group learning, as for international studies and liberal education, has been added unto that base, an extension of Extension, a secondary superstructure which under recessive pressure would be the first part of the structure to fall. The original purpose of industry is no more education than is that of commercial television. Labor unions, like churches, have moved toward the goal of helping build general intelligence, from an original goal of helping to build a convinced and effective membership. And the dedication of membership associations is to parts of a total social and educational goal, not to the whole of it. Nor would any of the organizations I have named even claim that their primary business was the achievement of general adult enlightenment.

Of the explicitly educational institutions, as we usually think of them, the library's primary work is the building of good collections of books and getting them into the hands of readers: an educational service, but not an education. The school, college, and university exist to serve the schooling of young people; and the university, in addition, to conduct research and develop scholarship to serve the minds of all men. The primary purpose of University Extension is to make the undergraduate curriculum and its professors available to people away from the home campus, to make available to the state the richness of the university's resources of knowledge and research. In every case, the service of purely adult learning is a late and left-handed service of the institution.

Second: Each of these institutions is staffed by people professionally trained to serve the institution's *primary* function: organization, librarianship, pedagogy for the young, scholarship or research; not *adult* education as such.

The report on *Adult Education Activities in Public Libraries* lists thirty-seven educational functions of the library. Eight are the supplying of books, booklists, audio-visual materials, and space. Nine are informing, advising, helping plan, about what the library can do and about what other agencies are doing. Eight are training, chiefly in storytelling, book reviewing, and reading, with two items on the training of discussion leaders and group participants, a very moot function in most libraries, actually. The remaining twelve, under "Doing," include book reviews, the making of library resources available to other groups, the program use of materials within the library's own collection, co-operation in radio or TV programs, making studies of adult educational needs and resources, and other really intra-library staff activities. Most of these are accepted parts of librarianship, and have their appropriate training in library schools. Most of them are also characteristic of larger urban libraries only. The library that launches an active program of adult group study, for example, is by contrast extremely rare; the librarian who can lead groups, and is willing to, is in a very small minority of the profession. Librarians are neither recruited nor trained for the purpose of teaching; and I should not even care to guess how large a minority of them ever take part in adult learning programs on their own, outside the library. They are well informed; one can always go to the librarian to find out what cultural and educational activities are available in a strange town. But their real, and important, service is to the individual book borrower. The library is essentially a "casework," book-resource agency; and neither its staff nor its sponsors, be they public officials or private trustees, would be prepared in our time to launch the library into a full-fledged teaching career.

Schools and colleges are in the teaching business; but the report on *Urban Public School Adult Education* makes explicit their critical lack of people who are trained in working with adults, in understanding adult needs and community needs. The largest instructional groups in University Extension are from fields of undergraduate academic instruction, mostly in such specialties as history, social science, English, business administration, engineering, and education; and a substantial proportion of the part-time Extension teachers are retired. Real strides have been made by University Extension in recognizing the need to operate on an adult basis; but over the country, Extension is still a secondary arm of the university, not a primary source for adult learning. And even the wisest modifications made by evening colleges to meet adult requirements are still modifications of a pattern made for another purpose; and, like the adult annexes of all the other institutions, are the most vulnerable to the pressures of expanding undergraduate needs or declining financial resources. For they are still subject to officers and trustees whose original and major goal must still rule their value-choices under stress.

Reflect further that when Councils and Associations are made up of, and dependent upon, representatives of these institutions alone, no fresh program or vigorous policy emerges. Only those staffed by professionals in adult learning have succeeded in adding a cubit to the stature of local programming.

Mind you, I have not forgotten that this is a conversation. And at this point I hear you saying, "How can you claim on the one hand that these agencies are doing great and necessary services for adults, and getting better all the time; and on the other that they *can't* do the job? What job can't they do?"

I do indeed say that these agencies are great and indispensable members of the adult educational team; they have been among the prime movers throughout the history of the movement, and will continue to be its most active agents. I further maintain that experience has brought them a growing measure of wisdom about adult methods of operation.

What I am saying now, however, is that their own existence derives from another purpose; that their staffs are trained for that other purpose; that the primary identity of each is independent of that of the rest; that they only *happen* to be together in the adult field because each of them has assumed some role in adult service as a secondary function; and that *you cannot build a coherent program of adult learning, a genuine plan or institution or service for adult intelligence, out of a chance collection of secondary functions branching off from primarily non-adult or non-teaching agencies.* Something new must be added.

Part Three

AREAS OF ADULT LEARNING

CHAPTER *7* *Discusses Education for Citizenship*

> The great problem of all civilizations is the creation of citizens: that is, of people who are dominated by the idea of the general welfare. . . . How are we to organize society so that people will not be in conflict with one another, will not nullify each other's efforts, but all will conspire together for unity, so that none shall be forgotten or oppressed or left out of our brotherhood?
>
> —AE, *The National Being*

> There are times I almost think
> I am not sure of what I absolutely know:
> Very often find confusion in conclusion
> I concluded long ago.
> —The King of Siam (*The King and I*)

No one, except perhaps political speakers, throws around as freely as adult education does such sweeping terms as "citizenship" and "community." They are the cant language of every statement of purposes, and every appeal for funds. It is this area of performance of public responsibility that was listed first among our "adult life-tasks"; and the Fund for Adult Education, in setting up the institutional studies, asked every respondent to specify what was being done in four fields, of which three are in this same area: "International Understanding for

97

World Peace; Strengthening Democracy; and the American Economic System" (the fourth was the Humanities).

When we begin to analyze the responses, to try to assess the actual effectiveness of our efforts in these fields, and to set this against a realistic view of American public practice, we suddenly realize that things are about to get a little rough.

Adult education has never attempted to set up controlled observational experiments to determine the effectiveness of its programs. We are left with a mixture of assertion and exhortation from which to try to develop some evaluations. Even religion is doing better than that: Baltimore, in October, 1955, was treated to a film-lecture from the Religious Research Foundation of Los Angeles, demonstrating the effects of prayer on plants over a three-year experiment: "It has been scientifically established" on the basis of 900 unit experiments with 27,000 seeds, the speaker explained, "that prayer can make an objective, visible, measurable, repeatable difference in the speed of seed germination and in the rate and vigor of plant growth." Perhaps citizenship education has been overlooking a bet; but if it has not tried prayer, it has tried almost everything else. The problem is to measure the objective and repeatable results.

The heart of the political process, as of the economic, is in the *decision-making* function. Differences between political systems can be strung along the line, "*Who* makes *what* decisions *about what?*" Democracy, ideally, supposes that *the citizenry control the decisions by which they themselves agree to be controlled.* Institutionally, our republic separates decisions into various areas, some functional—lawmaking, execution, adjudication—and some geographical: local affairs locally decided, interstate affairs federally decided, and so on. In theory, adult education prepares citizens to take their part in the making of the decisions that affect their living in the city, the state, the nation, the world. In practice, there is real question as to what levels of decision-making the average adult participates in.

One of my friends in San Francisco, on this trip, contended that in modern America there is less and less need for individuals to decide anything at all. The American goes to a job that found *him*, over a route prescribed by someone else, does what he is told, and comes home to supper, television, beer, and bed, without having controlled a single moment or factor, of any significance, in the whole process.

"I doubt, in fact, whether any of us really *make* any of the important decisions at all," he said.

"Like, 'How do you choose a wife?' " I suggested; and Bob, who is a bachelor, grinned and said, "That's an extremely good question."

I know what Bob means. But the fact remains that decisions do get made, on a hundred levels, in millions of places, all over America, every day. I suspect that few of them are individual decisions. Most of them are reached in small groups, and then presented or proposed to the larger group: the family, the trustees, the board, the local union, the city council, the senate, the membership. Every minute of every day, small groups of Americans are arriving at decisions.

My own postulate, as this bears on adult education theory, is this: that the decisions that affect the largest numbers of people, over the largest areas of their living, have been made by people who generally do not take part in adult education, who are in a sense immune to educational programs because they are too deeply involved in the power structure to take time for them or to give much credence to them. Your top executives, your political bosses, your senator, your city councilman, and your lobbyist are seldom seen in study groups or classes. They may have taken night law courses or accounting when they were younger; but in their decision-making heyday they are deaf to your invitation.

Adult education for citizenship, then, is left with two populations. One is that of *informed spectators,* whose approval or disapproval has some influence; the other, that of *influence-groups* that mediate directly between interested voters and the deciding interests. Let me take a specific example, the Citizens Planning and Housing Association of Baltimore. It has four jobs to perform: getting information, both about facts and needs and about people or groups whose interests or concerns can be involved in improving blighted areas; disseminating information through public meetings and mass media; forming and leading citizen committees that develop policies and recommendations; and focusing this interest on the Mayor and Council in a way that will lead them to respond appropriately. And the CPHA is credited with a very real role in Baltimore's renowned rehousing movement.

This suggests three steps in the education of the citizen about an actual issue. One is to get him to *care* about it; one is to get him to *follow* its development in actual events; and the third is to help him find ways of *expressing in action,* of some sort—of any sort, his concern.

For information and attitude-building about local problems, most of us rely most of the time on the press, followed by radio and—oftener on national issues—television. The channeling of this information into *caring about* is frequently accomplished in local discussion groups. These are of two major sorts: the discussion which is *incidental* to the ongoing program of a women's club, service club, YMCA, YWCA, community center, or other association whose primary end is not civic action; and the action-oriented discussion of associations of *focused interest*—of which Baltimore's CPHA is only one out of hundreds of examples. Press information and club discussion may serve to feed people into this latter sort of association; but, in general, only the latter sort is geared to help them find channels of action.

The last decade has seen growing emphasis, leadership, and skill poured by adult educators into helping resident groups within a city help themselves by concerted civic or political action. This new field of "do-it-yourself citizenship" is comprehensively known as "community development," and became in the early fifties the object of considerable contention within the adult education movement. Before considering its methods and values, however, I should like to set the stage by considering some of the problems that confront the effort to get people to "care about" and to "follow." Some of these problems are well documented in a thoughtful and carefully organized report on *Young People and Citizenship,* prepared for the Fund for Adult Education by Edward B. Olds and Eric Josephson, on behalf of the National Social Welfare Assembly.

Twenty national associations helped in this study. They range from the Collegiate Council for the United Nations to the Association of Junior Leagues, and include Catholic, Jewish, and Protestant bodies as well as Boy and Girl Scouts, Urban League and NAACP, Community Chests, and the Agricultural Extension Service. The problem was to find out what these organizations offered to young adults, ages 18 to 30, what characteristics of the young adult group seem to determine their response to these offerings. The specific connotation of the study was the preparation for citizenship, either by study or by volunteer activity.

Thirteen of these organizations reported a total young adult membership of a million and a half, with 98 per cent of them in the "building-centered" agencies such as the Y's, settlements, and community centers, and the Scouts and Agricultural Extension programs, and Junior

Leagues: "only about 5 per cent of the total U.S. population 18 to 30." Most of these organizations referred the questionnaires to their locals; and the locals found difficulty in translating their actual programs—social groups, forums, discussion clubs, and so on—into terms of the specific fields of citizenship concern that had been asked about. Nevertheless, the final estimates from the six largest organizations were that these matters had been considered in about 43 per cent of all meetings, with the heaviest emphasis falling on local civic affairs, ranging from garbage problems through delinquency to election issues. Types of meeting in the Y's ran heavily to classes, in the Extension Service to discussion groups, and in the Junior Leagues to leader and volunteer training sessions. The heaviest proportion of participation, however, came from board members and already-involved volunteers, with general memberships represented by only some 12 per cent of their number.

The principal conclusion reached by all who shared in this study and in the discussions that accompanied it was that young adults are (a) preoccupied with the achieving of and adjusting to adult status: mating, job finding, home establishing; "personal, social, and economic adjustment"; (b) denied participant status in the affairs and organizations of the community; and (c) unsure of either their need or their ability to "make a difference" by entering actively into civic affairs. In addition, it was felt that the agencies themselves either tried to attract numbers by stressing social and recreational programs, into which it is difficult to "inject" social problems; or tended to set up their own notions of what would be "desirable" programs and then to interest people in them, rather than going forward to meet the actual and pressing interests of the young adults themselves.

This brings us back to the notion of the changing nature of life-tasks in the successive decades of living. At

18, you worry about the draft; at 28, about the rent; at 38, about whether Johnny can read. Not only your status, but your *stake* in the community changes, and with these the foci of your concerns. This is reflected again in the report of the Council of National Organizations, which finds that organizations serving the ages 18 to 30 are primarily youth-serving, health and safety organizations, educational, and religious groups. Organizations serving the middle ages (30 to 55) are primarily in fields of women's interests and professions, politics, government, civil liberties, health, community service and community planning, education, industry. The organizations serving the ages 55 and over are primarily in fields of politics and government, women's interests, health, community services, business and industry. The middle ages receive the most primary attention and represent a wider variety of interests.

Attention to "strengthening democracy" was claimed by 60 organizations, to world affairs by 50, and to economics by 41. The order of rank in numbers of meetings in public school adult centers is world affairs first, then democracy, then economics. In University Extension, while "it is not possible to fit traditional university subject-matter classifications into the major-interest areas," it is estimated that world affairs rank first, economic affairs second, and "political understanding" third. Labor education is paying more and more attention to labor's stake and status in international affairs, and has the added incentive of increasing use of union members on international bodies and in exchange of persons. Industry, reporting some educational activity along these lines, at least in the larger plants, is rather frank about the intention of its programs: in economics, "an attempt is made to identify the employee's welfare with the company's profit situation," to show "the need for high employee productivity," and the role of Government as that of facilitating rather than hindering the operation of the free market. "Socio-political programs, on the other hand, are most often characterized by topics that have reference to government behavior and desired citizen reaction toward it."

In rural areas, Loomis' study of Rural Social Systems and Adult Education found well over half of all reporting agencies—schools, Extension Service, service clubs, farm organizations, women's clubs, P.T.A.'s and governmental program bureaus—indicating activities in the three fields. The predominant method was by public meetings with a lecture; "group discussion" was reported favored by a few agencies, but this may include questions after the lecture. "Small groups" were in a very small minority.

I am stressing the factor of *method* because the problem of citizen development is one of changing attitudes and practices: getting people to care, to follow, and to act. And there is a mounting body of evidence that this happens with some educational methods far more than with others. Specifically, the experimental work of Lewin and Bavelas, in farm women's groups, clinic groups of mothers, and groups of industrial workers, has shown consistently that group discussion followed by group decision, or by individual decision expressed in the group context, has from four to ten times the effectiveness of lecture and public explanation-exhortation, both in immediate *change* of practice and in the *duration* of the change.

Millions of Americans, in other words, are getting into the adult education statistics by having their ears dinned with speeches on public affairs, sponsored by recognized organizations. While we have not, as I said, enjoyed the benefits of controlled observation in any large way, I myself would not place the probable educational effectiveness of all these lectures taken together at more than about 5 per cent. That is to say, I doubt whether one person

in twenty went away with any change in his perception
of himself, of the social and political system he lived in,
or of the interrelations between the two.

The lecture audience comes and goes one by one, in
privacy of mind, just as the radio listener or the newspaper reader does. But long experience shows clearly
that it is chiefly through the opening up of the mind to
other minds, by free interchange, that growth or alteration of thinking takes place. If a thought or action process is already going on, a lecture may be useful in informing it or giving it a new depth of concept. But the
significant trend, both in rural public schools and in farm
organization programs, is toward the active *involvement*
of the audience in the process of public thinking.

The adult may be aware of conditions that need bet-
tering, but may not connect it with himself, may not see
himself as having any role to play in it. This is one of
the most frequent explanations of "apathy" given by ourselves and by foreign observers such as Gunnar Myrdahl,
who finds our culture deeply characterized by "strong
and competitive leadership and weak followership." And
this is also precisely the joint in the individual's armor
through which the point of education may pierce, to prick
him into action by giving him the sense of his own individual influence.

This has been known longer by ward bosses than by
educators. The word "influence" has been used by them,
too—but in a somewhat different sense. And here arises
the critical point about education for democratic citizenship. The ends for which the free citizen acts must be his
own, not someone else's. That is, if the citizens are to
create controls, they must be such as they themselves
want to be controlled by, must represent the values by
which they choose to live.

Let me try an example, to see where it will go; I am
not yet sure, myself. Take "fairness" as a value. If you can

convince the American that something *really* is not fair,
he will grow restless about it. Convince him that discrimination against faiths or races is not fair; then give
him a channel to express his restlessness through: a National Conference of Christians and Jews, a B'Nai B'rith
Anti-Defamation League, an Urban League; give her the
Council of Jewish Women, give them a committee on fair
employment practice. They will act, they will work, they
will move themselves by action in the direction of their
values, and so gain courage for their convictions. Convince the American woman that the isolation of mental
patients in inadequate hospitals is unfair; get her to volunteer her services, through her woman's club or church-
women's council to work for improved mental health
standards; show her how she can call on her legislator
at budget time: Maryland in seven years has rejuvenated
her mental hospitals by dint of such citizen action, with
press support.

The report on *Young People and Citizenship* also points
out an important, if subtle, distinction that American organizations like to make: they will not, for self-protection,
take positions on "political" questions; but they will take
stands on "public affairs." The League of Women Voters
does not endorse party candidates; but it will show its
members how to support legislation for better schools or
housing. This distinction itself is thought by many to
have an effect in creating "apathy": if the organization is
afraid to take a political stand, (a) why should I serve
it, or (b) who am I to take one by myself?

On the whole, however, the refusal to make party commitments has been wholesome. Organizations that do so
have tended to agree on only one: they are all against
bloody revolution, though they may disagree on where
that is likely to come from. The real reason, however, is
the one I have already stated: the true goal of citizen

action is not partisan, but the enforcement of values essential to democratic society—such as "fairness."

Most people are very concretely minded; and so "fairness" is most easily translated into action when it is seen in very specific local terms; and most of all when it is Me and Mine that suffer unfairly. "It isn't fair for our children to have to cross railroad tracks to get to school, when those on the North Side have an overpass." Around this specific, an alert leader can create an action project; and if his goals are primarily those of education, he can make out of it a learning opportunity as well as a chance to show, by a success experience, that apathy is not the only answer to resentment. Out of such opportunities has grown the community development approach, as practiced, and ardently preached, by such men as Richard Poston and Saul Alinsky. A broader approach has been that developed by the Ogdens, Howard McClusky, the Earlham group mentioned earlier, and the university-led programs in such states as Michigan, Pennsylvania, Wisconsin, and Indiana. In this method, community leadership is identified (no mean task in itself) and encouraged to define its own focus of need and interest, and is then helped to develop ways of self-help by which the community can take arms against its sea of troubles.

In a larger city, the "community" may be a single neighborhood. In one case, a nearly isolated development inhabited by nine hundred industrial workers and their families approached an adult education leader with a plea for help. He held three meetings with them, out of which forty volunteer interviewers were selected, trained, and sent from door to door with three questions only: "What do you think should be done in this neighborhood? Who do you think could do it? What will *you* do?" The results were assembled and presented to a further mass meeting, to which candidates for mayor and city council were invited, just before elections. "Then," said the educator,

"I step out of the picture, because I don't get into the action angle of it." As he said, "We ourselves are not an action-oriented program. We think the steps in action are two-thirds education and one-third running around the community getting the jobs done. Ours is the two-thirds. We take care of the heart and the head, then other people look after the hands and the legs."

Community development is not just anybody's vehicle. It calls for skill and sophistication of a high order, as well as unusual qualities of patience, persistence, and devotion. It calls for precision in recognizing the local power-structure, and the neighborhood patterns of leadership that can be aligned within or against it. It calls, as Jess Ogden has brilliantly shown,[1] for precision in timing. Therefore, it has tended to become the full-time preoccupation of certain educators, and they thereby have tended to become a separate group within the movement. This is what leads to controversy; and that, in this case, has taken the form, "Is local action really education?" And out of that question, in more recent years, several new insights have added stature and integration to the whole concept of the adult learning experience.

Explaining why the 1955 Conference of the Adult Education Association was devoted to this topic, the editor of *Adult Leadership* wrote: "What are some of these facts? First, that we Americans have become a nation of specialists. We are formed and molded much more by our association with others sharing our particular vocation or our particular leisure-time interests than by association with members of our geographical neighborhoods and communities.

"Second, that, because of specialization of interests and associations, we are losing our ability to communicate

[1] Jess S. Ogden, "Change Takes Time," *Adult Leadership,* IV, 1, May, 1955.

with one another about interests and problems related to the geographical areas in which we live.

"Third, that since family life and citizenship are carried on largely within the boundaries of geographical units— precinct, ward, village, town, city, county, state, and na- tion—there is a need to make our functionally specialized interests and group associations relevant to the life and problems we share with our neighbors and fellow citizens.

"Fourth, that the foundations of psychological and social stability and balanced growth are rooted in the degree to which our special functional interests and activities are related to our common interests as people and citizens.

"Fifth, that although furthering community develop- ment is not the *sole* business of adult education, it is an essential one if the American dream of participating re- sponsible citizenship is to be made real under today's conditions of extreme fragmentation of the community into special interest groupings.

"Sixth, that liberal adult education—the education of men for *freedom*—requires the actual practice of working with others in the processes of identifying the common good with respect to a multitude of specific problems and taking action to bring it about." [2]

In an article about the Conference, Cyril Houle, of the University of Chicago, said: "The leaders of community development are now (in their turn) in the process of realizing that it is not enough just to want to improve a community or to have an idealistic conception of what the good society is like. . . .

"But it is easy to see how in the earlier, more enthusi- astic days, the belief could be held that the immediate problems of the community are the only proper starting- points for adult education. The whole line of the argu- ment will become familiar to you if I quote its most re-

[2] *Adult Leadership,* IV, 4, October, 1955.

sounding platitude: 'You have to start with the people where they are.'

"Now those who use this sentence usually think they know where the people are. If they do, they are deceiving themselves. Each person is an individual. Also, he is not merely a member of a particular local community, but of a state, a regional, a national, and an international community. More than that, he is a member of a community which is not bound by time or space, a community of minds which stretches through the centuries. We must in truth begin with the people where they are, but that does not mean we must always start in the local community. Millions of people are reached each year by countless other approaches. . . .

"The true end of community development, as of all adult education, is to make life better by changing people in desirable ways. In every local situation in which people are free to act, there is a great power for good which is realized when they fulfill their capacity to deal creatively with their problems.

"What we want was suggested by Guizot when he referred to 'the energy of local liberty.' We need to free this energy which now lies latent and to use it to help people achieve better lives. The techniques of community development are among the most powerful ways by which we may hope to do so. . . .

"The improvement of our society is the aim of all adult education and not of community development alone. But that improvement cannot be achieved unless we use as well as we can the techniques which the leaders of this new field of endeavor are trying to perfect." [3]

Another useful summary is that of Leo Molinaro, executive of the Adult Education Foundation of Akron, which has also worked in this method among others.

[3] Cyril O. Houle, "The Energy of Local Liberty," *Adult Leadership*, IV, 7, January, 1956.

Molinaro said to me: "All this is preliminary, helping people to get the know-how. In this kind of work you do get visible results, and that cheers an adult educator even though you can't call it 'liberal adult education.' The next step is for me to go in there with liberal adult education. Right now, they're becoming a community; but more important, they're becoming *educants*. You have to prepare your consumer. Before the guy got in and drove the car away, he had to learn how to drive; he even had to think he *could* learn to drive.

"I feel the same way about the average adult citizen. TV and radio and newspapers, he thinks they're for him. He can find his way around in them, he's got plenty of *elbowroom* when he deals with them. He gets to a book; it begins to get a little tighter. He has to accept conditions of the author that he doesn't quite understand or agree to. You get him into a group, discussing ideas, and it's even tighter. The *emotional* elbowroom even is cut down then, other people's feelings are impinging on him. Finally you ask him to become a discussion leader—the situation is *really* structured then!

"But these are steps, and we've got to take them, one at a time. I don't hold with the adult educator who thinks that if he can get people to go on building sidewalks the rest of their lives, that's good enough."

In addition to civic action as such, there is another level of action open to, and followed by, adult education leaders. This is the attempt to enrich the programs of already community-interested organizatons (local or national) by two means: bringing them together for mutual enlargement of ideas and goals; and giving direct help in the development of program richness and leader strength. To a Junior Chamber of Commerce asking for leader-training, one Midwestern educator said, "What I want to suggest is that you fellows become *junior statesmen* of the community. Instead of the usual 'How to conduct a meeting or plan a program,' let's have a 'junior statesmanship training program.' Make it a kind of 'graduate' course, in place of the 'undergraduate' ones you've had before." Molinaro, in Akron, helped develop a ten-session course on the community for Junior League volunteers, at the end of which they take a test and indicate their choice of roles within the community.

All of this, of course, still assumes the local community as the content and the horizon of educational effort and citizen action. As to the role of these action-centered methods within the whole educational effort, Molinaro said: "I happen to think that *urbanization* is *the* most telling phenomenon in our modern America. I think it's determining new kinds of municipal policies, new kinds of politics, new kinds of economics, new kinds of human relations. America is producing cities, and city living, faster and more intensively than almost anything else. Adult education can begin, I think, to project a rather magnificent image of what life can be like in an urbanized, industrialized America. We've got to make life livable, make it *humane*. It's not a salvage operation, it's a 'salvation' operation that says, 'Tomorrow can be terrific!'

"How do you restore a human scale of measurement among the stone and concrete canyons? It's got to be done, to preserve the *quality* of life. The dangerous thing about 'automation' is that people begin to think it can be used to substitute, rather than to *implement* human desires.

"The city at the present time is a giant that's lying dismembered. Its head and its heart and its arms and its arteries are all in the wrong directions. We're astride this giant, for better or worse. We've got to put him together and make him work for us. Adult education can say, 'Here's where the city is irrational; here's where city life is rational.' There are great institutions in the city—the university, the library, the social agencies and civic organizations. They are tremendous links in a chain that hasn't been connected yet. Adult education can say, 'The connections can occur if you will talk with each other about problems of mutual interest, in politics, in economics, in world affairs or the arts.' The approaches are just as varied as people are. But it isn't enough to pick up a few dedicated precinct workers out of an institute. That's more than nothing, of course. But what really *liberates* these men and women is to know that they are working for a much larger concern than just the immediate issue."

In a brief article in *USA Tomorrow*,[4] Molinaro describes a two-day institute on Community Leadership in which "the traditional subject matter of the liberal arts and humanities were projected against the specific dynamics of urban life. Basic philosophical, historical, and psychological questions of values were examined and discussed within a framework of parenthood, social problems, economic problems, and foreign affairs. The symposium was a fulcrum balancing on the one hand the persistent concerns of Western Civilization, and on the other hand the modern, complex dimensions of the special problems which industrial urban America must confront." A statewide meeting of the Ohio Planning Conference was held in collaboration with the League of Women Voters. Architects, builders, and public leaders have met in study groups. The Mayor, the University, the City Planning Commission, and other members of decision-making bodies were involved in influence-making policy meetings. "Our hope," writes Molinaro, "is that with periodic assembly for deliberation and discussion among community leaders of this kind, there will be established a network of communication . . . which will make it possible for all interested citizens of Akron to take part in the process of

[4] Vol. I, 3, 1955.

city planning at whatever level they find appropriate to their interests, capacities, and energies. It is our conviction that a truly liberal adult education in the twentieth century must be a process in which the persisting problems of the ages in man's struggle for freedom of the mind and of the spirit are continuously and imaginatively recast in terms of the urban frontier. It is at this frontier that the problems of government, of human relations, of cultural and educational progress, and of economic stability will be determined."

Now let's look at another community that is being helped to learn its own needs and its own resources for dealing with them. San Bernardino, California, is one of eight growing cities and towns clustered within a valley just out of easy reach from Los Angeles, and within uneasy reach of each other. They are growing together, but against the obstacles of differing county and city provisions for service boundaries and differing controls over public facilities. To this cluster, Eugene Johnson and his associates in the Community Education Project at San Bernardino Valley College have applied a fine new word, "Metroplex." Here again, the guiding educational thread is "Man in an Urban Environment"; the guiding purpose is to get people, in formal and informal groups throughout the area, talking together about ways of handling their common problems, and to draw together the officials, the unofficial leaders, and the interested citizens into a great continuing conversation.

"Cities are here to stay. It is time to stop bemoaning their evils and to develop their possibilities. The improvement of cities is a major tool for improving the entire society. The social and cultural climate of the city will be affected" by events and decisions made at a distance, in the larger society of which it is a part; but "local citizens possess the opportunity to exercise a large influence (perhaps the major one) on the climate of their city.

"What kind of education must a city provide to enable its citizens to perform their roles in harmony with each other and with democratic values? What kind of education will cause people to want to participate in creating a new design for daily living in the city of today?" Again and again, in the committee minutes I am quoting, appear the themes of "values, communication problems, and the decision-making process"; and the question, How are the facilities of city living "scored" or "orchestrated" for "a triumphant symphony of daily living"?

The principal educational means have been a unique combination of mass media and intimate discussion. When a series of discussion programs has been written by the originating group, they are presented over several radio stations, each using a different time so as to spread the opportunity for listening. The San Bernardino *Sun-Telegram* publishes an explanatory article preceding each week's program; and from seventy-five to a hundred groups of listeners gather in homes and clubs to follow their listening with discussion, either without a leader or with one of themselves as informal chairman. The groups then report back to the originating office the trends of their discussion. In the fall of 1955, the radio program was put on twice in the same night: at the early hour, the content program was broadcast to the listening groups; at a later hour, the program went back on the air to hear directly from the groups what questions or conclusions they had to offer, and officials, appropriate to the topic being discussed, were brought in to the later broadcast to enter the discussion or to answer questions. In addition, daylong and week-end conferences are held, at the college or at an attractive resort, where officials and planning groups and listening-group leaders can work over again the important themes that have emerged in the discussions.

I hope I have not implied that Akron and San Bernardino have any monopoly on originality and energy in the promotion of civic communication. The enormous success of the "Johnson plan" of co-ordinated press-radio-TV-home discussion programs, adapted by the Foreign Policy Association to its project of involving citizens in "Decisions: USA" and tested in Oregon and Washington during 1955 and 1956, gives strong evidence that the mass-directed, multi-pronged, group-encouraging program will generate genuine power to develop an effective public opinion—not a "climate of opinion" but a *weather* in which small political craft will respect storm warnings. "Even complicated choices frequently rest in the end upon an act of judgment quite like common sense, and upon value-judgments which are in the long run the domain of the people." [5]

I have given this much attention to Akron and San Bernardino because they represent the types of most active and enterprising program, with a guiding philosophy of "creative urbanism." But they also raise some interesting questions.

One is the question I raised over the Earlham College program. The students working in community development projects were doing it as part of a planned educational program to which their other studies could be related. The townspeople were not. The experience of developing one's own civic know-how is novel, and may have a great deal of creativeness in it. But what about our curiosity and comprehension? How far are civic actors led to an understanding of the actual power structure of their community? Of the constitutional framework within which citizen action is made possible? Of the forces in our economy that work on their chances for success? What understanding do they gain of the dynamics that underlie group participation, or the motives that

[5] "Workshop on New Approaches in World Affairs Education," *Adult Leadership*, IV, 9, March, 1956.

moved themselves? And when we talk of implementing values, we are in a realm that has occupied philosophers for centuries; do we Americans now take certain values for granted, without the long hard work of questioning, of examining, of studying, of thinking—together?

Both the Akron Foundation and the San Bernardino Project make available a number of reading-looking-listening discussion courses: in parenthood, in the American heritage of ideas, in the ways of mankind. It would be of considerable value to know whether the people in the civic action programs also turn up in the discussion groups, or whether there are different kinds of people in the two kinds of program.

The Ogdens, similarly, hope in each community they help that they can leave at least a residue of citizens who will go on into the study of deeper and wider issues, of which their local experience will become illustrations rather than the whole content of their political wisdom. I believe this hope is characteristic of the best leaders in civic learning. But hope, even backed by University Extension resources, is not enough. There needs also to be provision for the intellectual excitement of head-on contact with the underlying ideas and issues by which men, from Socrates to the Supreme Court, have tried to understand their intentions and their obligations within a structured and humane society. This is not just "highbrow stuff"; as has been shown in hundreds of reading-discussion groups, this is the stuff of the intellectual maturity of the free citizen, the tough and intimate and exciting and perduring realm of choices of principle and belief. As I have said, we *do* think about these things, we do have opinions, we do argue our philosophies, however inexpertly. What is needed is a wider invitation to include other thinkers along with ourselves, an opportunity to discover how well they have said what we think, or to be shocked by their clarification of what we thought we thought.

Let me cite just one current example. A reading-discussion group on World Politics, in Chicago in 1947, proliferated into many groups in the Chicago area. In the next year, a partnership among the World Affairs Council of Cleveland, the Cleveland Public Library, and Western Reserve University brought the program into that city. Called the American Foundation for Political Education, and first hosted by the University of Chicago and the Chicago Council on Foreign Relations, with the help of a grant from the Fund for Adult Education in 1951, plus aid from at least one other foundation and fees from its participants, this program now has study groups going in a hundred cities and towns (including Akron), under the local sponsorship of universities, libraries, public schools, service organizations, or citizen groups. Well over six thousand men and women attended more than three hundred and fifty groups, even by 1954. For what?

Three courses, of ten meetings each, are offered: one in World Politics, one in American Foreign Policy, and one in Russian Foreign Policy. Each course is based on selected readings from classical and contemporary sources which offer a balance of contradictory views on persisting issues of policy. Readings are held to a reasonable norm of around fifty pages. The materials are furnished in sets, printed and boxed, and every participant has his own set of readings. Groups are held to around twenty or so, with two co-leaders who have grown out of earlier groups and received additional training.

My own predilection for this kind of study warns me not to try to discuss its merits here. All I want to point out now is that here, at one end of the gamut of citizen education, stands inquiry, through the interaction of minds within a group, into the universal issues and practical policies that illuminate the citizen's grasp of national and international political behavior. There, across the circle, stands the provision of occasions for enlisting the community-member in learning and *acting* on his own behalf. One side of the great arc between is filled with the nationally inspired programs of political study and influence by labor groups, women's groups, religious organizations, and the rest. On the other arc of the circle lie the immense offerings and resources of universities and colleges, of Agricultural Extension, of the public libraries: the institutions that can be pressed into the service of the inquiring adult if he, and they, so choose.

In this endless smörgasbord of political learning, then, are there any common commodities, any consensus on dietary values and good eating habits and principles of nutrition?

The "feel of the field," as I get it from the literature and from conversations, is something like this:

1. A majority of adult Americans are "inert" to political thinking and unused to political acting. This is not a class phenomenon; many of the inert are college professors and scientists, for example. A reasonably large minority can be attracted to interest in this area either by programs involving self-study of their own most immediate problems and organization to influence action on them, or by exploiting the emotional and intellectual impact of either local or international pressures. The armor we have to pierce is compounded of the unconscious conditioning and indoctrination all Americans receive as they grow up within the State; their unconsciousness of the State as a focus of intellectual issues; and the apathy that results from thinking either that politics do not affect them or that they cannot influence politics.

2. Information is the first line of attack; but information is ineffectual by itself, because (a) it is likely to be biased to support a partisan position, or (b) the indi-

vidual has no matrix of general understanding or interest within which to place or use the data given. Most people, it must be remembered, only read in the paper about events they already know about or have a frame of reference for. The politically inert population may have an avid interest in Ted Williams or the British royal family's romances; the problem is to deflect the area of interest into realms more appropriate to adult concerns. Information alone will not do this; most of what is given is not retained, according to frequent studies of this subject.

3. Self-interest can be utilized in the formation of influence-groups; and *influence* is almost always a *collective* undertaking. Here, the citizens need professional help in acquiring *know-how*. "Unconscious influence" is not worthy of the free citizen. Unless he knows how things happen and knows what he is doing to make them happen, he is less than free. Self-interest here is not a degrading term. In fact, it may mean that the individual has chosen among his many interests, say as between low taxes and good schools, and chosen the latter as the more "enlightened."

4. *Inquiry,* as against influence, is a pursuit of the individual. But he cannot pursue it alone; for only free interchange of opinion, free and unforced public debate on issues, values, and meanings, can open to the citizen the road to responsible decision. Therefore there must be, and can be, groups of people discussing the basic ideas of the political ways of mankind. This is the area of "know-why," instead of merely "know-how." But they are not antagonistic. The problem is to get them to coincide.

5. Because both influence and inquiry are public and collective undertakings, and because the decision-making function is nearly always, in a democracy, discharged by *groups,* it is in the group form that both influence and theoretical inquiry must be *learned.* The movement, therefore, is away from audiences, and toward groups;

away from speeches, and toward discussion; away from doctrine, and toward the confluence of different forms of *expertise* and different realms of interest.

6. The interest-group, the pressure-group, persist; adult education has no part in them. Its only commitment is that of free discussion, free inquiry, free association for purposes of study of all elements of the political problem. If the adult is to perform his public function, is not to be silenced and maimed in this most mature of functions, these commitments of adult learning must be fulfilled. No higher charge is laid by democracy upon its teaching institutions than this—that the free citizen is to be given the utmost help and encouragement in learning how, and why, to *control the decisions by which he agrees to be controlled.* This means both inquiry and action, and always by and in groups, under the best professional leadership we can muster. It means constantly increased and deepened channels of communication, such as adult education knows how to open. It means expenditure of time, energy, creativeness, and money; and never will education confront a better bargain.

Above all, it means that schools and libraries are "public" in a sense more important than merely that they are free and open to all. A truly *public* library is one that has recognized its obligation to help create a genuine public, in the democratic sense: a people capable of governing themselves. The public school or college is not "public" because the people support it through taxes; rather, the people support it so that it can enrich their wisdom in dealing with the public's affairs. In this sense, of course, the private institution may have a "public" mission, too.

These are not my personal pronouncements. They are the voice of the best men and women in adult education across this country; and they carry an overtone of crisis. It is later than you think; the time is now; only by urgent alertness can a free citizenry take, and hold, the moral leadership of a world on the brink of disaster. I would not, myself, urge the philosophy of "learn quick or die"; it tends too often to make a mockery of the education that is aimed at survival alone. What is needed is a broad national awakening to the vital importance of political enlightenment: in the words of Charles Farnsley of Louisville, "to put the tools of the twentieth century to work for the ideas of the Enlightenment": for Reason and for Man.

CHAPTER 8 *Discusses Education for Family Life*

> "Home is the place where, when you have to
> go there,
> They have to take you in." "I should have
> called it
> Something you somehow haven't to deserve."
> —Robert Frost,
> *The Death of the Hired Man*

> . . . I must go forth,
> Be father to my children
> And husband to each wife
> et cetera, et cetera, and so forth. . . .
> —The King of Siam
> (*The King and I*)

EVERY MARRIAGE is both polygamous and polyandrous. There is the marriage between a wage earner and a housekeeper, which has rather different dimensions from the marriage of one lover to another, though the partners are the same people. The son of this man, with his conditioned expectations about manhood, is married to the daughter of that woman, with her conditioned expectations about womanhood. This mother's son is habituated to certain feelings toward women, certain opinions about what a husband should be, what a mother does. That man's daughter has her counterparts of these habituated feelings. All these people, and more,

123

are trying to adjust to one another within a single marriage.

Even without their parents, and before any children, there are—to adapt a notion of Harry Stack Sullivan—eight partners in a marriage: the husband as he thinks he is; the person he thinks his wife thinks he is; his wife's idea of him; and her notion of the person *he* thinks he is. Add the equivalent four for her; and then conceive of the problems of *communicating* in terms of these "ideas." "I saw my son dancing with an Idea," says the god Angus Og in James Stephens' *The Crock of Gold*, "and I said to him, 'With what do you dance, my son?' and he replied, 'I make merry with the wife of my affection,' and truly she was shaped as a woman is shaped, but it was an Idea he danced with and not a person." [1]

We have taken it for granted of marriage, as of education, that it is something one "gets," to keep—or to exchange for another one, in the case of some marriages. But we know, when we reflect, that this is not so; that a marriage is made, not in heaven, but made and remade in each moment, in each decade. Havighurst and his associates, in the Kansas City Study of Adult Life, have made some tentative formulations of the role that husbands assign to their wives at different ages, as found in interviews with a goodly number of "normal adult males in business" at ages 30, 40, and 50.

In the words of William Henry, a member of the Study staff, "For the thirties the male is clearly seen as the central force in the environment, from whom all action stems. He is almost invariably 'right' and his confidence is seen as solving all problems. Yet the male here is not a particularly busy or involved person. Rather there is low interaction for him and between him and the female. For these men, the female is essentially a foil to the goals of

---

[1] James Stephens, *The Crock of Gold* (New York: The Macmillan Co., 1954). Used with permission of the publishers.

men. She follows the cues given her by the men. She is strongly emotional. She gets upset and hysterical. The men can and must cajole them into line. The interesting technique is for the man to take the blame for any difficulty. The woman can control only through the giving and withholding of love and sex.

"In the forties the men become more uncertain and skeptical about the husband-wife relationship and see it as full of trouble and difficult circumstances. They lose to some extent their image of the man as strong and competent. The female now becomes touchy, irritable, and 'female.' . . . It is important, however, that all these men agree she must be lived with.

"In the fifties the woman for the first time becomes a person with her own goals and plans. Interaction takes place as between two real people, rather than categories and stereotypes of people."

Other fluctuations are being studied along with these, of course. Concern with his body, for example, preoccupies the man in his forties more than the one in his thirties, they think, while concern with emotion, love, and sexuality is less.[2]

These observations are not meant to imply a norm for all male attitudes within those age ranges. I cite them here only to remind us that the roles of spouse, parent, provider for aging parents, and their related roles in the cluster of family functions, are matters of continual readjustment, and subjects for lifelong curiosity, creativeness, and comprehension. They constitute a prime function, and a stiff test, of adult maturity.

Education for marriage and family life, including both child development and family problems of the aging, is not one of the older branches of adult learning; but it has

[2] William E. Henry, "Affective Complexity and Role Perceptions," in J. E. Anderson, ed., *Psychological Aspects of Aging* (Washington, D.C.: American Psychological Association, 1956).

come along strongly in the last decade. In the Baltimore public evening adult program, a whole department is devoted to it, with day and evening discussions, evening courses on marriage and human relations "especially for fathers," pre-school and school observation trips followed by discussion, and television and radio programs on child development. Parent study-discussion classes, and a pre-school "parent training center" in which the parents attend a kindergarten session once a week and have an evening meeting of their own once a week, are offered by the Sacramento Junior College.

In San Francisco, where ten years ago only seven parent education classes were offered in a year's time, there flourishes today a full-scale Family Life Education Service, under the public schools' Adult Education Division. Initiated in 1950 with the help of a grant from the Rosenberg Foundation there, the Service now provides study-discussion groups in connection with twelve co-operative nursery schools; for parents of children in an assortment of school grades; in connection with Child Care Centers; workshop courses in how to develop the child's interest and activity in art, music, reading, and listening; courses in making the home itself more attractive and more secure; psychology courses for "the middle years," for families with working mothers, and others; marriage preparation classes; leadership training for family-life program groups, professionals, and volunteers working with children and young people; and a variety of workshops and conferences bringing individuals and organizations into communication around these common themes.

In San Bernardino, one full season of home-listening radio-discussion programs was built on "The Years Between," the problems of transition from adolescence to young adulthood: leisure, gangs, the draft, family problems. An index of the effectiveness of these programs is the number of teen-agers who attached themselves to these groups which had been planned for adults. Most of the seventy-five home groups had some young people in them, most successfully when they were in other homes than their own. Only one who has tried to develop mixed-age groups knows how rarely it happens, and what an electric contribution the younger ones make to the whole discussion.

Akron was trying out with four groups an experimental course on "Parenthood in a Free Society," prepared in Chicago and furnished by the Fund for Adult Education on a trial basis. "One group was all West-Enders, well off, above average incomes, good schools and some college, professional and high technical levels. How they would discuss the feelings of security and adequacy is so different from the groups in other sections of town. Interracial groups in neighborhoods with great economic differences and tensions; different, but no less valid," Leo Molinaro said. "The beauty of this program is that it turns the parent back on himself. It doesn't offer any formula by which the parent can manipulate the children. If the question is security and adequacy, it becomes 'What makes *you* secure?' In talking about democratic goals and values in the family, it asks, 'What do *you* consider democratic values, and how do *you* teach them?'

"One group we divided into mothers and fathers. I took the fathers and I said, 'What values do you think fathers can teach to children that mothers cannot teach as well?' We made a list: sportsmanship, fair play, the usual things you think of a man handling. The mothers came back, and they said the greatest thing they could teach to their children was respect and love and understanding of fathers! The fathers were embarrassed to death because we had included no such thing in ours. Talk about quick marital readjustment! The mothers were disappointed in us fathers because we didn't come up with that insight—a very tender and important insight."

Parent and family life topics are given "major attention" in the curricula of twenty national membership associations, ranging from the Film Council of America to the Girls Friendly Association and the Universalist Church; "moderate attention" by eighteen—health associations, youth agencies, professional institutions; and "incidental attention" by six. Experience tells us, however, that these good intentions translate into local programs chiefly where strong local interest is organized around one or another phase of the subject by local agencies: mental health groups, Family Life Councils, Extension Service, churches, or schools.

Never until our own generation was the role of parent so laden with guilt and anxiety, among educated adults. Some of this stemmed from the popularity of Arnold Gesell's books on the behavior characteristic of children at half-year steps of age from birth to adolescence. Young mothers in thousands of neighborhoods became a "Gesellschaft" whose members anxiously watched their own children, consulted the book, and compared notes with each other, ignoring Dr. Gesell's own warning that no child exactly meets any norm of development.

The popular spread of psychiatric theories about child development and "problem parents" immensely increased the load, until almost the standard question asked by mothers in parent classes became "What did I do wrong?" A growing reliance on professional pediatrics paved the way for acceptance of psychiatric mysteries, with the common assumption that there was only one "right" formula, which the despairing layman could never master. I know one psychiatrist in Baltimore who still insists that no parent can be trusted to guide the growth of a child without the explicit direction of a psychiatrist.

The corrective began to make itself felt as pediatricians relaxed their formulas, as Benjamin Spock brought comforting reassurance to millions of mothers, and as psychiatry began to realize that it was frightening more parents than it was helping by its earlier forms of parent education. Around 1950, the Group for the Advancement of Psychiatry, a vanguard movement within the American Psychiatric Association, turned down a munificent gift of free radio time in fear that any attempt at mass psychiatric enlightenment would only lead to an overanxious population of listeners.

The strong emerging trend in parent education, in the current decade, lays its emphasis on self-understanding and on becoming "comfortable" within the parent-child relationship. This has meant turning away from formulas, from intellectualized instruction, and toward informal group communication among parents under sophisticated and sympathetic leadership. Its goals are to free the parents from formulas and stereotypes, to free their curiosity to explore the real child with his needs, his strengths, his capacities for change and growth; to give the parents confidence in their own ability to find creative avenues of relationship; to enlarge their comprehension of the forces in human development. In Molinaro's perceptive phrase, the goal is to help parents to achieve the "tender and important insight" whose place no instruction, however expert, can take.

Home skills, household economics, the principles of nutrition and hygiene, and many other arts are ancillary to this main line of learning. They, like the vocational arts, are well mastered by our teaching techniques. The new and significant movement in family life education is along the lines of relationship awareness, and thus becomes part of another of the adult's responsibilities: self-understanding.

When significant changes are taking place in the structure or composition or process of a complex civilization like ours, it should be one of the major responsibilities of adult education to help the members of that culture absorb, interpret, adjust to, those changes. The automobile changed the structure of our suburban countryside without benefit of inquiry; even driver-safety education for the young is a recent addition to our curriculum. Automation is getting more lip service than interpretive study or discussion. And the changing proportions of the population to accommodate increasing numbers of old and retired people have become of educational importance only within the decade.

In 1950, when the National Conference on Aging was called in Washington by the then Federal Security Agency, only 1 per cent of public adult education programs reported any activities for older adults. Among universities, the outstanding leader was Michigan's Wilma Donahue and the Institute for Human Adjustment at Ann Arbor, with a comprehensive program of institutes, courses, groups, and broadcasts for and about aging adults.

The Conference section on Education concluded that our society must "free itself from the traditional prejudices against old age and launch, through its various educational channels, a campaign to accent the positive characteristics of the aging for continued occupational usefulness, citizenship, and family life. . . . The task of modifying our institutions so that the aging population may remain integrated into the framework of society is fundamentally an educational one. This task . . . will require a re-evaluation of existing practices in all areas of society, a development of new and more varied educational techniques. . . . The paramount goal of education in altering attitudes must be that of bringing the individual to adopt an intelligent viewpoint toward growing old, interpreting the process of aging at each of life's stages as part of a purposeful pattern of living." [3]

What has been done in this field in the present decade is still little more than experimenting and exploration, along lines mostly recreational and avocational: clubs, hobby shows, and the like. Our cosmetic interest in covering the real problem is shown in the names we give such clubs: Golden Age, Senior Citizens, and the other terms to which my son once referred scornfully as "youthemisms." What courses have been tried on the vocational retraining side are characterized by one of my more caustic friends in public school adult education as "teaching retired carpenters bookkeeping and retired bookkeepers carpentry." There is some resistance to "segregating" older people into a population minority; and California has learned the dangers of this through a near *coup d'état* staged by the old folks a very few years ago. The goal of that coup was financial security; and this is likely to be the goal of old folks' political action until they have been given the broader security of continued integration "into the framework of society . . . as part of a purposeful pattern of living."

Altered patterns of housing, the preference of older people for keeping their own homes, and their gradual immobilization in them, suggest increased reliance on the mass media and neighborhood groups. The work of the Cold Spring Institute, which was mentioned earlier, has shown that physical and social reconditioning are effective in restoring bodily energies that were supposed lost, and social creativeness that had been neglected. During this exploratory period, I think there is urgent need for

[3] *Man and His Years:* An account of the first national conference on aging (Raleigh, N. C.: Health Publications Institute, Inc., 1951).

urban centers to which the older people can, in Arnold Toynbee's term, find "withdrawal" while they renew their energies and incentives for the "return" into their action stations.

In general, however, my point is that the preparation for being old and for living with old people is now a major part of learning the adult role; and hence, a major responsibility of adult learning. Here again, while a few pioneers are pointing ways, there is a challenge to adult education itself to develop curiosity, creativeness, and comprehension. Above all, the need is to communicate these three qualities of life's advanced students to us undergraduates who are not only treading out new paths, but also retracing the old ones.

The family role, in summary, appears more complicated than it ever has. And this is due to the fact that among the many changes we are aware of and can shrug off, the changes in understanding of human development and in the actualities of family living are moving faster than changes in politics, in social institutions, or even in industry. A major role of adult education in our culture is the mediation of change; and it is in the area of family relations that education has one of its stiffest challenges today.

Education for family life is still a minority field within the whole of adult learning in America. It is usually the concern of special-interest agencies; the universities have hardly touched it as yet. Yet this is the most intimate and most creative of all the *roles* the adult has to play within our culture. It cannot remain a minority interest, for it directly affects citizen performance, vocational performance, and the quality of American living as a whole. Today, it is still a weak link in our educational chain; but its strength is growing, and that growth is significant of the maturing of our educational vision.

CHAPTER **9** *Discusses the Relation of Education and the Job*

> The planter, who is Man sent out into the field to gather food, is seldom cheered by any idea of the true dignity of his ministry. He sees his bushel and his cart, and nothing beyond, and sinks into the farmer, instead of Man on the farm. . . . The priest becomes a form; the attorney a statute-book; the mechanic a machine. . . .
>
> —Ralph Waldo Emerson, *The American Scholar*

> The man coming to his daily task brings his family with him.
>
> —James Plant, *Personality and the Cultural Pattern*

IF ADULT LEARNING IS, as we have assumed, most securely attached to the identities by which the adult knows himself, we must recognize that a large part of everyone's identity is supplied by the occupation in which he makes his contribution and earns his keep. Ask a man who he is, and he is quite likely to tell you first what he does: "I am a bookkeeper" or a steam fitter or a salesman.

Where the task of training is one of improving his skills in his working role, the task of education should be that of giving a wider meaning to his *identity* in the role. For this is only one of his identities. He is also his family's head, his town's citizen, his church's communicant; and he does not stop being these while he is at work. But neither does he leave his occupational identity behind him when he attends to something else. Vocational training deals with him as a "hand"; here, we Americans have developed tremendous powers of imparting skill. It is as we think of him as a man that our approach to education about his work becomes hesitating and confused.

What should a man know about his means of livelihood? Well, does he know the role of his industry or business or profession within the nation's whole economy? within the world economy? Does he think about what his own work contributes to that industry, or business, or profession? Does he see himself in relation to those who work around him, over him, under him? Does he know the destination of the goods he handles, and what they will become in the hands of those who get them? (Or should he care?) Does he think about the variety of loyalties the job involves him in—to the company, to other workers, to the town, to consumers, to his country, to the progress of men in all nations? These are samples of what one might suppose would be concerns of the thinking worker.

The worker in industry has, usually, two memberships through which educational opportunities may be offered: the union and the plant. If the union can help him find the incentive, he can learn widely from its educational resources: not only bread-and-butter union matters, but the broad sweep of labor history, in which he can find for himself a creative role; the broad outlines of the economy in which he takes part as producer and consumer; the broad picture of international affairs, particularly as they affect labor itself and his company and his town, and are affected by these. As his local's representative in out-of-plant activities such as workshops, institutes, college courses, he can work at his understanding of human relations, of his community, of other countries; and at foreseeing the implications of automation, for himself and in the larger picture.

Management is also looking for ways to motivate him to learn: about the company and its needs and its beliefs about productivity and profits; about the theories of a competitive economy; about public affairs; and, again, about human relations. Above all, of course, the company wants him to keep up with the inhuman speed of technological change and innovation. Ever larger numbers of companies are offering wage incentives and course fees to tempt workers into evening study of advanced techniques in their fields—though the National Industrial Conference Board in 1956 reported that less than 5 per cent of eligible workers were taking advantage of tuition aid.[1]

But these are only two of the worker's memberships. And, curiously, both are having difficulty in developing adequate incentives to workers' learning. To cite Carroll Williams, business editor of the Baltimore *Sun,* "The failure of employees to fit themselves for promotion, for positions of a supervisory nature, and increased responsibility, creates a major problem for management. More and more companies are carrying on intensive promotional campaigns," including encouragement to non-vocational interests such as English, crafts, social activity skills, and pre-retirement courses.[2]

On the face of it, management has the best chance to reach the workers in the business or plant, especially on a released-time or shared-time basis. There is a growing interest in making the plant a sort of part-time school. But this, too, has its problems. As looked at in England by Harold Shearman, one of the very wise leaders of

[1] Baltimore *Sun,* March 14, 1956.
[2] *Ibid.*

British adult education, "There have been indications that some firms have become interested in the development of Adult Education for their employees. [But] if Adult Education is to contribute, as it certainly should, to the development of a virile citizenship, it should be set in the focus of civic and social responsibility. This means that the worker should be enabled to relate his own industry to the larger interests of society by mixing in study and discussion with those engaged in other activities. . . . It would be anti-social . . . if enlightened industry leaders set out today to make the works [3] the microcosm of the worker's life, cultural and social as well as economic, and thus helped to impoverish the wider society. . . . Adult Education should bring together those with common interests from the widest possible field, not merely those who work together, and should do so under conditions where there can be no question of freedom of speech and initiative being menaced." [4]

Management's executive employees are workers, too; and here, as I have said, there is a variety of patterns growing up for a general education approach, some in-plant, some away. Here, as with union classes, the core is of a bread-and-butter variety, stressing management itself in its various skills. And here, too, economics, international affairs, and broad liberal studies are being encouraged. But there is no evidence, as yet, that the executive group is headed toward an educational landslide either. "Executive development" has become a high managerial assignment; and company training directors are now numerous enough to form a national association and to consider steps toward becoming a profession. But incentive is still a problem.

At the heart of this problem, it seems to me, is the too-

---

[3] What we would call "the plant."
[4] Harold C. Shearman, *Adult Education for Democracy* (London: Workers' Educational Association, 1944).

ready assumption that one identity of a person is *the* identity through which he may be reached. From the point of view of the worker himself, the union is only one facet among his many identities; for the executive, the plant is only one. Either man may be drawn into some program as a library user; as a Mason; as his wife's husband; or as the father of school children. "Union loyalty" or company urging may be very real factors in the appeal of their sponsored programs. But it may turn out that *any* program succeeds only to the degree in which it involves *multiple* loyalties. This, again, suggests that local collaborative programs, urged by union, company, church, school, and press, have the best chance to attract people; and to work with them in terms—among others—of their occupational identities.

The educational task is to help the individual, wherever he may appear, to conduct an inquiry into the personal and social meaning of his labors, the social meaning and justification of his "take." If he cannot respect his job, respect himself in it, a large share of his total identity is left hostile to the rest of it. And if he does not understand it, he cannot know whether to respect it. Too many of us are apologetic about our jobs; the "dignity of labor" is an egghead's myth, until the job is accepted as one of the facets of life that is talked about in educational contexts. Economics discussion groups are such a natural context, and the discussions there reflect the occupations of the group. Parent education groups need to consider the effect of father's job, and the absence it entails; and the effect of mother's job; and the impact of work relationships on home relationships. In all manner of groups, discussing anything from *Studs Lonigan* to the intellectual freedom of librarians, I have heard members use their own occupations to illustrate an argument, and seen them use the group's ideas to illuminate their own vision of their jobs.

Adult education, in whatever form, has simply to remember that its client is a *total* adult, who works and plays and thinks and relates to his fellows; who requires a feeling of respect for his activities and of integrity in his performance. No segment of adult learning is remote from any part of the identity of this total person. Because they are the functions of one person, they are finally indivisible. If education is compartmented, it is the fault of the educator, not of life.

CHAPTER 10 *Discusses Education for the Enrichment of Living*

> I am interested
> In my feelings. I seem to wish to have
> some importance
> In the play of time . . .
> What is deep, as love is deep, I'll have
> Deeply. What is good, as love is good,
> I'll have well. Then if time and space
> Have any purpose, I shall belong to it.
> If not, if all is a pretty fiction . . .
>   the least
> I can do is to fill the curled shell of the
> world
> With human deep-sea sound, and hold it
> to
> The ear of God, until He has appetite
> To taste our salt-sorrow on His lips.
>   —Christopher Fry, *The Lady's Not*
>   *for Burning*

> Of Life immense in passion, pulse, and
> power,
> Cheerful, for fullest action form'd under
> the laws divine,
> The Modern Man I sing.
>   —Walt Whitman

ACTIVE CITIZENS, healthy families, and thoughtful workers make up the roots and trunk of the Tree of Liberty. But that tree dies that bears no flowers

139

and no fruit: and the fruit and flower of a free culture are in the mind and spirit of its people; in the familiar enjoyment of ideas, the rich perception of the world, the loving insight of the arts, the proud knowledge of their cultural and scientific tradition.

Yet it is precisely at this point that the widest gap appears between those who create and promote these areas of cultivation, and those who hold responsibility for the education of adults. "On the record," says Grattan, "it is clear that the managers of adult education have had least success in making these fields of interest continuously parts of their programs. . . . Certain it is that American adult education has had very little to do with the vast diffusion and acceptance of superior music in America. Nor can it be said that the vast increase of interest in painting . . . owes much to adult education. . . . Similarly with the humanities and the social sciences. Insofar as these have made their way forward in recent years as fields of interest for adults, the progress is more to be attributed to the writing activities of academicians and nonacademic intellectuals, than to anything adult educators have done systematically to sustain and promote such studies." [1] And from the artists' side, Robert Gard, the sensitive and passionate shepherd of the Wisconsin Idea Theater, writes: "The terms 'adult education,' 'institute,' 'specialist,' were terms of annoyance to me. I considered programs built through and around such terms to be noncreative, deadly, with a shallow general purpose of uplifting, without much emphasis on genuine human considerations." Yet "I sensed that America must come to her maturity through the cultural things." [2]

There is no evident necessity for such a gap. Grattan

[1] C. Hartley Grattan, *In Quest of Knowledge* (New York: Association Press, 1955), p. 305.
[2] Robert Gard, *Grassroots Theater* (Madison: University of Wisconsin Press, 1955), pp. 79 and 76.

guesses that "it is probable that if the administrators of public-school adult education had been interested in developing the liberal studies" (i.e., instead of assuming that the market was for vocational studies) "they would have found a responsive audience." [3] But the funds that made public school adult courses possible were, by Congressional choice, vocationally directed. The testimony of our libraries and museums, and the huge if still minority audiences for such television offerings as *Omnibus, Adventure, The Search,* and such Shakespearian programs as those of Professor Baxter on educational channels and of Maurice Evans or Laurence Olivier on commercial ones, suggest that there is a genuine and widespread cultural hunger for ideas, for literature, for science and the arts, which we are not nourishing in our institutional programs. The large-scale response to the musical and art offerings of the Louisville Public Library reveal that there is something approaching a mass audience for fine materials if they are made easily available; and librarian Graham and former Mayor Farnsley, there, have no less a goal than the "saturation" of their city with the enjoyment of the best that Western culture has to offer.

Now let me turn, in order, to the need, the opportunities, and the obstacles to humane learning and creative enjoyment as goals for adult education.

For the first, let me turn back to Mr. Nickerson, whom I have quoted before. He cites with approval the statement that "we need people with convictions reasonably and deeply held, the sane judgments which come from emotional stability, and the imaginative comprehension which comes from understanding the whole condition of man." Then he adds his own word: "Our business system, indeed our whole scheme of contemporary American life, requires the education of men and women of moral stamina who can think and who can discriminate

[3] Grattan, *op. cit.,* pp. 227–228.

among values. This implies the necessity for the continued extension of a sound liberal education." [4] Still quoting from business leaders, I turn to Gilbert Chapman, president of Yale and Towne: "There is a growing fear in the United States that we are facing as great a danger from internal ignorance as from external attack. Our advancing technology has fostered the rapid growth of specialization, and with it the intellectually incomplete man. . . . The United States has become a dominant power in the world, but she cannot for long exercise her power or fulfill her mission without our being a people literate, educated, and cultivated. . . . The specialist must also be a humanist." [5]

I have deliberately chosen my spokesmen from the managerial class rather than from the classic sources, because these are the men who best know the uses of specialization and the requirements of an industrial culture. But even the military show trends in the same direction. According to Raymond Thompson, writing in the Baltimore *Sun*, the new Air Force Academy has included a richer share of humanities and social sciences than its older rivals, on the view that "present concepts of warfare make it necessary to produce men . . . with a clear picture of the political, social, and economic factors that underlie the problems of our time. 'We are training generals, not second lieutenants.'"

And, finally, from the President of the United States, in a speech at Penn State in June, 1955, this statement: "We are not as proficient as we should be in providing a broad citizenship education to those who specialize in the many technical fields. And . . . even in liberal education, we have permitted it to become too much a specialization,

---

[4] Albert J. Nickerson, "Choosing and Using Industrial Leaders," *Saturday Review*, November 21, 1953.

[5] Gilbert W. Chapman, "The Opportunity Ahead," *Saturday Review*, November 21, 1953.

rather than a broad, liberating influence. . . . What we need is general education, combining the liberal and the practical, which helps . . . achieve the solid foundation of understanding—understanding of man's social institutions, of man's art and culture, and of the physical and biological and spiritual world in which he lives. It is an education which helps each individual learn how to relate one relevant fact to another; to get the total of relevant facts affecting a given situation in perspective; and to reason critically and with objectivity and moral conscience toward solutions."

Neither you nor I would dissent very much from these resplendent statements of the goals of learning. I am the more astonished, therefore, at what I have to say next: astonished that, in discussing a field called "education," it is necessary to argue in behalf of *knowledge*. Yet without it the goals of general education will not be reached. And in all honesty we are faced with two glaring facts: first, that Americans on the whole simply *do not know* what they need to know in order to enter what Grattan calls "the enduring world of adult discourse"; and, second, that adult education, apart from formal courses, has sought to achieve its goals almost wholly through the elaboration of process rather than the enrichment of content.

This is no longer the fighting issue it once was among us, for we have all learned that effective processes of interpersonal communication can add value and flexibility and focus to our use of the things we *do* know. Group processes have shown value in the modifying of attitudes, the acquiring of human relations skills and of self-knowledge. I am not belittling these achievements. But it is still true that in the arts, the sciences, history, literature, philosophic thought, and all the wonders of man's culture and enjoyment, the mass of the adult audience is dependent on what is given in newspapers and magazines, on radio and television: a flood of materials undiscriminated, unfocused, unorganized, and without any inherent power to help the adult himself learn how to discriminate, to focus, to organize. We educators, meanwhile, maintain our doctrine of "working with people where they are," by means of a variety of social processes; and too often go away leaving people where they were.

I may have appeared too solemn in listing the creative enjoyment of one's culture among the "tasks" the adult needs to master; or too frivolous in calling this the realm of "play," as against the bread-and-butter tasks. But I am quite serious in saying that we are in some danger of leaving "curiosity" to be satisfied by gossip, "creativeness" by a do-it-yourself kit, and "comprehension" by the mere acquisition of tolerance for other people's views. And while I have not lessened my faith in the value of good method, neither will I accept the contemporary belittling of intellectual *content*, the need not only for adult discussion but for adult *study*.

"In the college," I wrote some years ago, "we not only look for the development of liberal social intelligence; we also expect that development to come about through the use of books. How otherwise, then, should we pursue that same end with adults?" There is an answer, which includes materials for listening and for looking. But there is no answer that can exclude books as a major resource for learning. Libraries and University Extension list millions of book borrowers. But organized programs of adult study confess only a few thousand adherents among informal book-and-group programs; many thousands more in college-type classes. The statistics give one the impression that most adult programmers are content to leave *study* to the colleges and universities, reading to the libraries. But we have already questioned whether college class instruction is suited to, as it was not designed for, adult needs. The grownup uses books and arts and ideas in a different way, for immediate as well as more ultimate ends of his own. Why, then, has this kind of need and use not been reflected in a wider range of adult learning choices? Is it possible that adults are driven to take college courses, with or without credit, in the fields of liberal learning, simply because no one else is offering these materials in a more adult manner?

It is suggestive that "Humanities," of the four fields stressed in the FAE studies, loomed very large in reports from twenty-eight University Extension Divisions, totaling more classes than the three citizenship fields combined, with about the same enrollment in correspondence courses and about a third of the total of "conference" themes. Wisconsin alone reported fifty adult classes in art in 1955. University evening colleges are strong here, too. But the public school adult totals showed the Humanities with the fewest classes, and the smallest recent growth, of the four fields; though Loomis cites a table of public school adult courses in Michigan in 1952 with one in twelve falling in the arts, music, and drama. Of the public libraries, about one in ten—mostly in the larger cities— reported book discussions and fine arts programs. But less than one in six of the national organizations confess any concern with arts or humanistic studies.

Book discussion programs, including Great Books, the Foundation for Political Education, American Heritage, and a few independent ones—even in hospitals and prisons—probably together enlist fewer than one adult American in three thousand. But this is no indication of their potential. Some of the limitations arise from conditions of the programs themselves. Great Books is a fairly literal translation of an undergraduate program into the adult arena, with its closed groups, indoctrinated quiz-masters, and exorbitant pace of reading. For me, it emphasizes too much the acquisition of a chronological catalog of ideas rather than a muscular interplay of judgments and issues with one's group and with thinkers whom one has had time to master, to live with, and to make one's own. But this is only *one* possible pattern of adult study. What is significant is that, even within these limits, Great Books has survived to become the oldest established permanent floating book-game in the field.

A second significant discovery of these programs is that there is no limitation to an elite class in the enjoyment of "the mind's play and the mind's work." Longshoremen and machinists, bankers and scientists, alike find excitement in these programs. And perhaps the most significant of the universally familiar comments of college-graduate students in such groups is, "This is what I hoped college would be like, only it wasn't."

As objects of pure enjoyment, books and knowledge are ends in themselves. But, within the total enterprise of maturity, they matter mainly to the extent that they contribute to our own personal integration and enjoyment of being alive. Knowing "about" poetry is no substitute for the surge of one's own spirit on the passioned wings of Walt Whitman or Emily Dickinson. Knowing *about* the Constitution is no guarantee of the high achievement of informed citizenship.

The role of knowledge in learning was beautifully stated long ago by an English schoolmaster, William Cory: "At school you are not engaged so much in acquiring knowledge as in making mental efforts under criticism. A certain amount of knowledge you can indeed with average faculties acquire so as to retain, nor need you regret the hours you spent on much that is forgotten, for the shadow of lost knowledge at least protects you from many illusions. But you go to a great school not so much for knowledge as for arts and habits; for the habit of attention, for the art of expression, for the art of assuming at a moment's notice a new intellectual position, for the art of entering quickly into another person's thoughts, for the habit of submitting to censure and refutation, for the art of indicating assent or dissent in graduated terms, for the habit of regarding minute points of accuracy, for the art of working out what is possible in a given time, for taste, for discrimination, for mental courage and mental soberness."

It is to such "arts and habits" that knowledge should be dedicated if adult education is to develop into the "great school" of maturity.

On the side of opportunity in the arts, let me remind you of Howard McClusky's pointed remark, "Community development need not always begin with getting sidewalks. It can begin with a community chorus, an art center, a village band." In the little town of Wayzata, Minnesota, what had been in 1954 a small art class in a cellar room suddenly exploded into a whole set of adult learning activities, and while still housed in random rooms began calling itself an Adult Education Center and planning for a home of its own. Richard Crohn, of the New American Library, has argued that the adult center of the near future will be "a center filled with the opportunity for culture. The individual may come in for any purpose, a class in how to use a screwdriver; but when he comes in he will find himself in the presence of good pictures, of books, of music, of all the ways we have to satisfy his hunger for good things."

Thus far we have spoken, as with libraries, in terms of access and invitation. But what justifies a belief that an interest in art, for example, can open windows onto the vital areas of living wisdom? Here, let me cite a paper given to a section of the Adult Education Conference in 1954 by Irving Kriesberg, a young New York artist and teacher.

A work of art, says Kriesberg, is "a record of one man's feelings"; and the observer can learn to enjoy the color,

the line, the "areas of constriction and release," in terms
of his own responses to color and light and shadow, of
laughter and fear. He can see the individuality of the
transformation the artist has wrought upon nature: "To
distort nature is to bend it to an idea. To give a thing
meaning is to alter its raw or pristine state. Distortion of
nature is the inevitable result of human activity. To trace
the act of transformation in a work of art is to apprehend
the human mind in its most characteristic function," to
"learn how natural it is for men to transform their experience in order to give it meaning." The rhythms and energies of the picture then begin to release our own feelings: "Who has not felt at times an overwhelming desire
to scream—to blaspheme the corruptions and frustrations
inevitable in life?" If we do not, it is not merely because
of convention, but because "a raw scream has the feel
but not the truth of reality. But if we can have our cry
made true and beautiful . . . ! This is the pleasure and the
function of a Van Gogh canvas, to scream—with truth and
authority and with much more poignancy, because it is
so beautiful."

But beyond the individual insights and releases, there
is a more important function in the work of art: "Most
of us are convinced that the salvation of the individual
today is tied up with the salvation of society," and the
movements of art "give us insight into our society."
Renaissance artists recorded the new concepts of their
time, "the outward physical reality which was the passion
of the new man. They put their people in landscapes.
They bathed them in light and shadow. They created
such devices as vanishing point, perspective and fore-
shortening." But with the revolutionary changes of the
late nineteenth century came revealing, in fact prophetic,
changes in painting: with Van Gogh, Gauguin, and
Cézanne, "the whole edifice, constructed with such pride
and delight by the Italian masters, toppled. When Gau-

guin painted shadows blue and water red, he overthrew the principle of light and shade; when Van Gogh made every sky and field and tree a relentless self-portrait, he denied the principle of objective reality; when Cézanne adopted a multiple focal point in depicting a plate of apples, he rescinded the principle of optical perspective."

But at the same time "the blows of the other revolutionaries were all in the same direction. In painting, Cézanne and the Cubists ended the idea of the fixed focal point as a means of depicting reality. In music, the concept of a home key, a fixed point of reference, was challenged, and the range of tonalities and rhythms enormously expanded. In sculpture, space became as important as the solid. Different types of sculpture called transparencies, mobiles, and constructions replaced the concept of a stable solid.

"In physics, the idea of a fixed point of reference for measuring and computing was abandoned. Einstein's overthrow of the absolute laws of Newton was analogous to Cézanne's overthrow of the laws of da Vinci. . . . We have come in the same way to accept the psychology of the unconscious and some new truths about human motivation. We have come to look upon human society and morals and economics from a comparative point of view, abandoning, if you will, the fixed focal point.

"It is not coincidence that we adopt relative standards to measure distances and to judge societies. . . . Our age is of a piece. We are no longer surprised when we hear that science does not deal with an objective world of facts. We have realized that . . . science puts the question of reality aside" to deal with "working notions. . . . And like the physical scientists, our historians are telling us that 'facts' are not the simple, fixed, uncoverable things we once thought they were. . . . We have come to realize that the whole edifice of man's knowledge is . . . a struc-

ture of laws and ideas created with marvelous success by
man himself.

"The human brain is an organ which naturally and
constantly translates experiences into symbols and ideas.
The artist's translation may be infinitely subtle, infinitely
audacious, infinitely broad in scope. . . .

"Art does not solve our problems. Art does not even
state them in specific terms which might lead to a solu-
tion. But it can tell us where we stand. It tells us, from
deep inside, where we are. . . . Daily we look for signs.
One of the most dependable signs . . . is the United
Nations. Yet there is in a sense a more fundamental sign"
of what the United Nations stands for: "It is the building
itself. Think back on the buildings of the League of
Nations—those monstrous piles of Grecian columns! If in
the year 1920 men could upon clear ground build nothing
but these stale archaic structures, then it was plain—before
the events of Ethiopia—that men were unable to tran-
scend the past in order to deal effectively with the present. In 1950, the fact that men were able to create a
monument that breathes a new spirit—this in itself speaks
more decisively than do the delegates in the meeting
halls. And even if it does not say positively that we will
survive the crisis, it does give us the measure of our test;
it shows how great must be our leap if we are to survive." [6]

A great leap, indeed, to this many-splendored perception of our times that Kriesberg exemplifies. But how are
we to make the leap: on our hands? Tugging at our own
bootstraps? For the solid fact remains that most of our
present personnel in adult education is itself without the
kind of learning that we are asking them to impart. As
Kenneth Benne has written on the more general theme of
learning for maturity, "It seems to me that . . . all teach-

[6] Published, in part, in *Adult Leadership*, IV, 6, December, 1955, as
"Art in Adult Life."

ing to some extent, but particularly adult teaching, becomes the teaching of what we don't know. . . . I think we have to learn to teach what we don't know." [7]

The Overstreets in 1941, in *Leaders for Adult Education,* demonstrated that practically all the then leaders got into the movement by force of accidental circumstances: "some accident that has thrust new experiences upon them and has made them like these experiences." "One becomes a member of the adult education body simply by taking part in some enterprise that adds to the individual or social insight of adults; and one becomes a leader simply by doing one's part well enough. . . . No one of these people had his initial interest in adult education stimulated by any course he took in college. . . . No one of them was persuaded to become an adult educator by some other adult educator. . . . Each was already at work before he became an adult educator. . . . Each one acquired the skills necessary to him as an adult educator by a trial-and-error, on-the-job process. No one of them, having glimpsed the possibilities of the new field, thereupon took time off to return to academic walls and prepare himself for adult education."

In that year, the Oversteets were able to cite a few schools devoted to the training of adult leaders: George Williams College in Chicago, with its emphasis on community life; Springfield College, with emphasis on group work; the Merrill-Palmer School, emphasizing parenthood and family life. They noted that rural extension teachers were required to have expertness in one field, and a general sense of rural life. They cited the attempts at training workers' education leaders, and they called attention to the astonishing, if temporary, impact of WPA adult classes. They stressed also the growth of approved discussion group leader practices and conference leader

[7] Presidential address, Adult Education Association, 1955; published in *Adult Leadership,* IV, 7, January, 1956.

techniques. They recommended training for discussion
and conference participants, as well as leaders; and they
deplored the fact that "American adult education, in its
classroom phases, has suffered keenly from the fact that
most of the enrolled men and women do not expect to
do any studying outside of class," and the resultant failure to build up "that common background of knowledge,
interest, and reference which is always, for any group,
one of the richest rewards." They pointed out that many
non-readers might change their habits "if they encountered a different set of expectations on the part of those
who teach them." And they concluded that adult education "has the job of studying and experimenting with all
the types of adult experience that can hopefully be
counted upon to multiply in our society leaders and fol-
lowers . . . who honestly want to engage in processes that
will help them to know more than they do now about
life and what it requires of them." Elwin Svenson, in an
unpublished doctoral study done at UCLA in 1954, reviewing the somewhat more extensive provisions for professional training that today's adult educators may choose
from, cites twenty-five top authorities as agreeing unani-
mously that "the adult educator should, himself, be an
educated person."

Throughout the literature, however, it is simply taken
for granted that if a person has a particular field of instruction, he will be expert in that field, and will have
adult teaching skills added unto him. If he has no special
field of knowledge, he can lead by skills alone. I have
often, myself, argued that it is perilous for a man to lead
groups in the field in which he *is* expert. As Robert
Blakely puts it, "It is harder for a subject-matter expert
to keep his special knowledge in check than it is for a
layman to acquire the subject-matter orientation and discussion techniques to lead a group well." But a practiced
and organized grasp of a recognized field of learning is

not, in itself, a handicap to anyone who takes a hand in the learning efforts of others; and neither is a reasonable grasp of a broad range of intellectual methods, principles, data, and issues. In the words of Mary Follett, "It is not a knowledge of his specialty which makes an expert of service to society, but his insight into the relation of his specialty to the whole." [8] But this is precisely what we are supposing would be the goal of general education. And this brings us back, full circle, to our initial question: From whom are we to learn?

The students of the field whom we have consulted would appear, then, to have presented us with a dilemma: How shall we choose as between "process leaders" and "content teachers"? But I am quite sure that this is a false dilemma, one which does not really exist; and I shall be happy to give my reasons for thinking so.

First, let us agree that for many areas of adult learning there *must* be content to be learned. You would not have a group discuss art in the absence of pictures to look at, music without instruments or recordings to hear, or history and philosophy and government and anthropology without solid materials to grow on. We are well agreed also that these materials cannot be, in the ordinary sense, "textbooks"; for the textbook has already done for the student what we want him to do for himself. He cannot interact with a textbook. The materials he uses for learning have to be ones to which he can feel what I have called an "intimate response."

Second, I think you will agree also that what makes such materials really available to, usable by, grown-up students is the *social process* in which they get involved while using them. The adult seeking understanding about his own living does not want just a classroom; he wants, as I said earlier, "companions in the search for greater

[8] Mary P. Follett, *The New State* (New York: Longmans, Green & Co., 1934 ed.), p. 64.

wisdom." And the leader, if he is in a group of companions in learning, may be a learner too. He need not be responsible for what is in the materials; he must have some sense of responsibility for the process by which the members become involved in learning together. This is *adult* education.

The movement long ago discarded the term "teacher" in favor of "leader," in recognition of just these facts. I am not sure I would go all the way with this notion; it seems to me there is a place for teaching wherever there is a place for learning. But it must be most carefully redefined to shun all implications of texts and classes, and to emphasize the role of the senior student, already better acquainted with these riches, in companionship with others to whom he may give a good deal of help, but from whom he will also be truly learning. Like the public school students described by a U.S. Commissioner of Education years ago, we adults "go to school to books, and not to teachers." What we have to convince ourselves of is that the *leaders* of adult programs themselves need, and are able, to go to the same school.

The trouble with the supposed dilemma between process leaders and content teachers is simply that it makes the assumption of two separate sets of people without either interest or competence in each other's work. This is what is false. Adult learning at its best is a social process; and all of us who take some responsibility for it can and should be learning together the things we do not yet know but need to know, as adults ourselves and as educators of adults. Agricultural leaders, school administrators, club chairmen, librarians, college teachers—all of us share some realms of ignorance; yet if we had the nerve to pool our curiosity and our creativeness in the great search for comprehension, we should find ourselves leading a "revival of learning" that would put the Renaissance to shame!

Here, again, it seems to me that the task is essentially a local one. Tom Adam, writing of museums in adult education, complained that no educational organization outside the museums made planned use of the riches inside of them, but left the burden of educational programming up to the museum itself. The college that offers content courses to lay adults offers only "leadership process training" to the adult leader. A few cities—Dallas, Louisville, come first to mind—have taken music into the educational partnership, and fine arts as well. But actually all our cities and regions have all the resources needed for the liberal cultivation and enjoyment of our living. We who work in adult education, however, have tended more to promote their use by others than to become learners ourselves. And we have failed—whether through pride or through just being too busy—to *arrange to learn from each other.*

Finally, another answer to the "learned leader" problem is offered by programs which supply materials for the cultivation of intelligence but do not presuppose the need for a specially cultivated leader. The most familiar recent type of program in this field is what Cyril Houle has called the "co-ordinated program," such as those prepared or sponsored by the Fund for Adult Education. These are fee courses which supply to the members of a group the materials—in print, recording, film, or whatever is deemed appropriate to the presentation of the ideas—for ten or twelve weeks of learning together, with the group furnishing its own leadership on a rotation basis. The Center for the Study of Liberal Education for Adults adds the broader notion of the "focused study program," combining learning and life experiences in a planned and sustained fashion.

The variations around this point of leadership reflect the deep puzzlement and concern of the whole field. The Great Books program recruits would-be leaders at large, and gives them a fast trial run over part of the course they are to be responsible for. The Foundation for Political Education believes (as we did in the Washington Public Library program) that leaders must be found *in* the groups themselves, and encouraged to assume discussion leadership on the basis of certain demonstrated interests and abilities. The so-called "packaged programs" of the FAE's Experimental Discussion Project grew out of that staff's concern over the fewness of liberal-learning groups, and their feeling that their growth was "hampered" by the dependence upon skilled leadership, as well as by the lack of planned promotion, distribution, and financing. They decided that materials for discussion series could be prepared without the need for trained leaders; and on that basis prepared experimental courses in Economic Affairs, World Affairs, Art, Parenthood, the Ways of Mankind, the Jeffersonian Heritage, Ways to Justice, Introduction to the Humanities, You and Your Community, and others, with new ones still in preparation.

Professional participation in the programs was to be at the point of *origin:* each series "should be developed under the auspices of a recognized institution having a staff of special competence in the subject area." Programs "should be designed to be used in groups with volunteer discussion leaders, preferably employing a plan of multiple leadership." But "it is the hope . . . that . . . these programs will result in both the discovery and in-service training of volunteer leaders. . . . The Fund recognizes the need for the development of a growing pool of people with discussion leadership training and experience in every community." And "some provision must be made for professional and semi-professional assistance" in getting such groups organized and "managed."

But the professionals who arranged the materials began demanding that the leaders who used them be "approved" students of the field involved in the materials; especially in the areas of fine arts, music, parenthood, and economics. Experience, at the same time, was showing that what we vaguely call "background" has as much to do with a leader's success as does his skill in guiding conversation.

The issue of the educated leader is not a very substantial one. Glen Burch, the head of the Fund's Experimental Discussion Project, has never questioned the *advantage* of a trained leader. His question concerned the *necessity* of trained leaders. I should think the present agreement in the field ran along these lines: that it is important for the discussion group to maintain the sense of equality among its members, including the leader, who always knows less about some matters than do some members of his group; and that the amount of training and experience required for a leader varies with two other variables: the *precision* of the knowledge involved in the content (for example, in economic affairs as compared with a discussion of characters in a novel), and the *delicacy* of the interpersonal problems presented by the material (say, in a group of parents of problem children as compared with an economic affairs group). By giving to group leaders some additional experience as members of a group learning how to lead, and by the easily recognized device of attracting into leadership the people who have already been interested students of the material, the difficulties of finding effective lay leadership are minimized, and the necessity of relying on professors and experts is avoided. The related problem, of how to use "resource" experts within free discussion groups, is still, however, one that baffles all of us. Here, perhaps, is where the professional preparation of the materials for study comes to the rescue.

Returning to Houle, we find him attributing spectacular success to the army's co-ordinated courses in World

War II, and looking ahead to the employment of similar devices for liberal learning: "Certainly the principles of adult liberal education would appear to be capable of expression in a co-ordinated course. The mature person should expect to take charge of his own education. He should want to learn the best that has been thought or said or portrayed by those who have had the deepest insight into what he hopes to learn. He should realize that many minds have preceded his along the particular voyage of inquiry on which he is embarking and that consequently he should try to secure the very best guidance as to what he should read and in what order. To maintain his independence and vigor of viewpoint, however, he should use experts in both content and method but never abdicate to them. The mature person will often study independently, but he should also seek the stimulation of a group of like-minded people who, through discussion, can bring their different backgrounds to bear on common problems and thereby illuminate the understanding of everyone concerned. . . . The mature person always evaluates a program of learning in terms of the meaning it has for him and the group to which he belongs. Finally, he expects that any given learning experience should provide him with stimulus for further thinking, reading, and participation."

Pointing back to the estimated one hundred and twenty-two million copies of McGuffey's Readers that illuminated the school days of our grandparents—and that supplied thousands of raw teaching recruits with elements of a teachable culture to which they might not have had any other access—Houle suggests that the co-ordinated courses may become "as it were, a kind of McGuffey's Reader of adult education." To this end, "The central purpose . . . has been to give a large number of people a few basic concepts rather than to give a few people a large number of concepts." While the basic aim is to impart *knowledge* of the field under discussion, another objective "has to do with the development of leaders for our society. The experience of presiding over a co-ordinated course, of being for a time the first among equals in an exploration of an important topic, can have a significant influence on the development of community leaders." Quoting Lowell Martin to the effect that "the only formal teachers in the groups are the authors . . . ; the discussion leaders mediate between the 'teachers' and the 'students' by creating those conditions under which constructive group thinking occurs," Houle points out that the leaders must be "intelligent citizens who are well adjusted socially, have a warm regard for people, an objective respect for facts, and a natural inclination for positions of leadership." But he adds that the conditions of leadership should never "imply . . . that [the leader] has a superior understanding of the material on which the group is focusing its attention. His duty is simple but sometimes very hard to perform: he must so conduct the discussion that the group and its individual members enlarge and deepen their own understanding of the subject."

Yet in the next breath, Houle raises the hard substrate of our problem: "Will co-ordinated courses serve their purpose only until trained and professionalized leadership is developed?" And he also suggests his own answer: "The co-ordinated course embodies very basic beliefs about adult education: that the students are mature, that they can conduct their own education, that they will want to be aided by high expert guidance, that they need to use . . . various media of communication . . . , that they find learning more profitable in groups. . . . These beliefs must surely underlie any sound program of education for the mature. . . . If the aim of spreading understanding to many people be a desirable goal, these principles or something very like them must be used. In no other way can the democratic hope for universal adult education be achieved."

Here, I assume, Houle is speaking not only of the Fund's "package" programs. He is thinking of all kinds of study groups using materials of learning, within the very broad field which I have called "the creative enjoyment of life." He is not minimizing the wide range of materials that can be used for learning; and he concedes that "the loyal adherents of books sometimes seem like the chiselers of stone and the copiers of manuscripts." But he also adds that "reading permits a depth of study which radio, the films, and television can achieve only under extraordinary circumstances." His conclusion is to be taken with complete seriousness: "In this generation there are, in fact, two central tasks. One is to broaden the base of participation and the other is to increase the depth of learning of those who take part. . . . In the accomplishment of both of these goals, the use of print plays a central and essential part." [9]

But widening the use of print among adult students will require widening its use among adult leaders and teachers: this is the simple and unescapable conclusion. It is for those who plan and train for program leadership to find ways of lifting the levels of preparation and widening the horizons of "background," without making prigs and pedants of their pupils. It is, I think, only as all of us who work in the adult field begin ourselves to acquire the habits of learning together that we shall become honestly and appropriately able to create the wide interest, to project the broad programs, of which we dream on behalf of others.

It would be too much to say that the movement that

[9] All quotations from Houle are from his chapter, "The Use of Print in Adult Educational Agencies," in *Adult Reading*, Fifty-fifth Yearbook of the National Society for the Study of Education, Part II (Chicago: University of Chicago Press, 1956), pp. 157–187. Used with permission of the National Society for the Study of Education.

began in order to remedy the educational deficiencies of its clients needs now to attempt the same service for its practitioners. Rather, what I would say is that the enrichment of living through knowledge and enjoyment is still a basic desire of all adults; that we in the field, being adult, share that desire; and that we have the means, if we have the courage, to join our fellow students in achieving it, together.

CHAPTER 11 *Discusses Education for Self-Understanding*

so many selves (so many fiends and gods
each greedier than every) is a man . . .
—how should a fool that calls him "I" pre-
sume to comprehend not numerable
whom?

—e e cummings

Men—creatures who can be held together
only with the greatest difficulty. . . .

—Sigmund Freud,
New Introductory Lectures

To a young man caught in a woman's bedroom by the woman's husband, remarked Joseph Wood
Krutch, it is a matter of some importance whether her
husband is addicted to reading French farce or Western
melodrama.

If "we are what we read" seems too strong a postulate,
I would still contend that the *self-picture* on which we
base our behavior is drawn from the reflection in us of
people whom we have made important: living ones are
most important, but characters projected and approved
by our familiar culture-groups have their importance too.
You can read the change in a whole nation by the changes
in its gallery of heroes, as the depression audiences of
the thirties saw Dos Passos turn Joe Hill and Gene Debs

162

into heroes and Rockefeller into a sorry jest. The young adolescent builds his life-dreams on heroes; and the adult still looks for himself in human mirrors.

"Know thyself," as a maxim of adult education, is attributed to one of the earliest practitioners of the art. Like other ancient teachings, it gets no easier by the mere virtue of its familiarity. The individual in today's confusion of cultures has perhaps the hardest job that any civilization has set men in this way. While few of us would subscribe to psychiatrist Frankwood Williams' exuberant statement that "until 1890, nothing was known about human nature," I do think that we in our generation have access to more dynamic insights into human behavior than were available before. And we are under an urgent obligation to use them. Education has too long suffered from the mere *assertion* of values, often based only on traditional practice and belief. One way we get over being children is by discarding assertion in favor of *investigation,* discarding tradition in the light of newer knowledge. If adult education is to grow beyond its prolonged infancy, I think we should begin to challenge the repetition of old forms and beliefs in the light of newer psychological insights. With all due respect to "adult psychology" in the terms of the Thorndike school, I believe that adult education, in the middle of the twentieth century, must take seriously the dynamic psychology of the ego, the self-picture, and the desperate struggle to organize that fragile collection known as "the personality."

This has, in fact, been the intention of Group Dynamics, as well as of those of us who have ventured into mental hospitals and clinics and jails to search out the processes *within* people that determine the relations *among* people. This, too, is why I would now bring into our conversation Carl Rogers, the University of Chicago's advocate of "non-directive" counseling. In a brief talk to a 1952 Harvard Conference on influencing human behavior in the classroom, Rogers said, in part:

"It seems to me that anything that can be *taught* to another is relatively inconsequential, and has little or no significant influence on behavior. . . . I realize increasingly that I am only interested in learnings which significantly influence behavior," which means "self-discovered, self-appropriated learning. Such self-discovered learning, truth that has been personally appropriated and assimilated in experience, cannot be directly communicated to another. As soon as an individual tries to communicate such experience directly, often with a quite natural enthusiasm, it becomes teaching, and its results are inconsequential. . . . As a consequence, I realize that I am only interested in being a learner, preferably learning things that matter, that have some significant influence on my own behavior. I find it very rewarding to learn in groups, in relationships with one person . . . , or by myself. I find that the best, but most difficult, way for me to learn is to drop my own defensiveness . . . and try to understand the way in which his experience seems and feels to the other person. I find that another way of learning for me is to state my own uncertainties, to try and clarify my own puzzlements, and thus get closer to the meaning that my experience actually seems to have . . . as I try to understand at least the current meaning of that experience." Rogers himself states, in some pretended alarm, the implications that would follow: "We would do away with teaching. People would get together if they wished to learn."

Again, I am skeptical of the total rejection of "teaching." The "teacher" has at least the function of contagion; the reading group, as I once wrote, learns from "the liked leader" to like the authors and their companions in the group; and liking precedes learning, which can only come from *friends*. But there is no present point in semantic quibbles. The point of Rogers' statement is quite plain, and quite pertinent. Learning comes from one's attempt to make meaning of his experience, which is best done in company, and its test is an alteration of his response to others.

The notion of multiple *roles* played by each adult has become familiar in all discussions of education. What I am concerned with now goes somewhat deeper: it is the notion that there are many *persons* within each adult. I do not mean complete individualities; I mean "person" in the simple sense in which we ordinarily use it: do you, for example, present the same person to a dining-car acquaintance that you present to your cleaning woman? In a committee meeting, are you the same person you were while you were alone in your car, driving through traffic and swearing at other drivers?

In this sense, "person" means a certain more or less coherent set of ways of responding to others within a particular situation or relationship. Farmer Jones is progressive about his dairy herd, but very stubborn with his children. Principal Smith is quite democratic in the Rotary Club, but autocratic with his teachers. Mrs. Martin and her mother are on very good terms—except when the children are there. I myself used to wonder why I could discuss political questions so reasonably with my students, only to get helplessly angry over the same issues when I was home arguing them with my father.

I use the two words "discuss" and "argue" very deliberately; for the difference between them is both a good illustration of my thesis and also an important measure of the educational process. I have told elsewhere the story of "The Colonel Who Joined the Group": a man whose role in a reading-discussion group had for the first weeks been that of arguing, of turning every point into a controversy, until he had got tagged with that role by the whole group. One day, a few weeks along, he astonished all of us—including, I think, himself—by raising a question about something said by the man across the table, and adding quite earnestly, "I'm not just trying to win an argument. You evidently see something that I don't, and I'd like to know what it is."

How shall we describe this man? I think of him as one who had been exploiting a truculent self, for what advantages it brought, and who had let another, more questioning and reasonable self get rusty, until somehow the *invitation* implicit in the group's method had brought it to the surface and given him *support* in employing it again. As William James once remarked of religion, "I am sure that in many cases of conversion it is less a new truth than a new power gained over life by a truth always known. It is a case of the conflict of two *self-systems* in a personality up to that time heterogeneously divided, but in which, after the conversion-crisis, the higher loves and powers come definitively to gain the upper-hand and expel the forces which up to that time had kept them down in the position of mere grumblers and protesters and agents of remorse and discontent." [1]

We are misled, you see, in thinking about the "individual," unless we remember that he is also a "Dividual," a cluster of identities which he has derived from the other persons he had to respond to in growing up. If this sounds too atomistic, let's put it in the terms Harry Stack Sullivan sometimes used, borrowing the phrase from William James: that, by growing up in dynamic interrelation with a number of different but significant people, the human being develops a "self-system" which is a cluster of *habits of responding* in certain ways to certain *types* of person or situation. Outside of this more or less organized Self-system by which each of us seeks the world's approval

[1] *The Letters of William James* (Boston: Little, Brown & Co., 1926), Vol. 2, p. 57. Permission to reprint granted by Paul R. Reynolds & Son, New York.

and co-operation, other systems of response may also exist without our being very clearly aware of them, though they form real and operating parts of our "personality." These are response patterns that we have learned are too costly to practice openly, so we "dissociate" them, shove them out of sight, down into some cellar of our being.

"The traditionally emphasized individuality of each of us, 'myself,'" says Sullivan,[2] is "the very mother of illusions, the ever pregnant source of preconceptions that invalidate almost all our efforts to understand other people." Each of us "conceives himself to be a self-limited unit that alternates between a state of insular detachment and varying degrees of contact. . . . When he uses the pronoun 'I,' he includes in its reference only those motives of which he is aware" or about which he has information. Now, what I am saying, in addition, is that even within this selective "self" there are several rather different pictures which he tries to act out in response to a variety of other people or situations; but some part of what he is trying to project for other people to see, some part of what he is trying to prove to himself, has its roots in a level of motivation that he is not conscious of acting on. And some of the "persons" he thinks he is dealing with are, in fact, illusory.

The adult as we meet him in education has formed his "selves" into some semblance of order. They are a club, with rules; they have chosen one of them as president and elected a public relations committee. In sum total, they present a "personality," a "character." Then, as we watch him in his several roles and relationships, we begin to sense the many selves, and to ask which of them we are planning this education for. Finally, we begin to recognize *a person in quest of himself,* trying to find out

[2] All quotations from Sullivan are from *A Study of Interpersonal Relations,* Patrick Mullahy, ed. (New York: Hermitage Press, 1949), p. 98 ff. Copyrighted by Thomas Nelson & Sons, New York; used with permission.

who he is and what he is, what he should do and why he
should do it. Through the multiple forms and facets, we
suddenly see what is the real substance of learning: this
endless vital process of *Becoming*—of becoming ME, amid
the welter of "I's" and "me's" and "you's" and "they's"
and all their shifting interplay of give and take. As James
Stephens says,

> *But he,*
> *The self,*
> *The Watcher of the race,*
>
> *The One,*
> *The Witness,*
> *Knower of the plot,*
>
> *Who bears life*
> *As a mask*
> *Upon a face—*
>
> *He goeth not!* [3]

Education, since Dewey, has liked to use the word
"Growth"; but this too easily assumes that all Becoming
is an advance. Becoming may also be a diminution, a
leaving out, a warping. I can become *less*, as measured
along any of the myriad parameters of humanity. But
becoming I cannot stop, cannot avoid. At every moment—
at this moment—each of us is, by his experience and by
his use of it, making himself more, or less, or different.
Mostly we repeat, we sustain last moment's totality. But
also we have the freedom of what Whitehead beautifully
calls "the creative advance into novelty": by this act, this
thought, this awareness of a feeling, we shift the balance
of our inner forces so that the next step falls slightly to
this or that side of where it might have gone. We make

[3] James Stephens, "Theme and Variations," *Collected Poems* (New
York: The Macmillan Co., 1954). Used with permission of the publishers.

ourselves different by the bit of difference our action makes.

The raw stuff of experience is *prehension,* the taking hold of events by our senses, our feelings, our intuitions. The goal of learning is *comprehension,* the making of sense and unity and purpose out of that raw material. The trick, of course, is in the doing; and this is just what we learn from other people. A "person" develops out of, and *only* out of, give-and-take responses between himself and those around him. His very conception is an interpersonal act; his initial substance comes from another; his earliest nourishment is at others' hands. By the time he can even discriminate among the people around him, he is well on the way to some of the persons he may become. Some think the first six months may determine the schizophrenia he may suffer much later, just as they can the rickets that will bequeath him his adult bowlegs.

To grow into a person, he must collect a variety of identities from identification of himself with those to whom he has intimately responded: those on whom he depends, and later a few significant others. The raw archaic stuff of perception and feeling gradually gets shaped into judgments, recognitions, fears, goals, values, and behavior patterns through his *internalizing* of other figures and through *projecting* them again onto persons and events outside himself. The *gamut* of his possible responses to people and events is the heritage of his dynamic relationships with the persons who formed the context of his growing up. The variety of his identifications, and their varying success and failure, reward and punishment, in successive social situations, make a continuous fluid puzzle which each man must solve for himself. But at the profoundest core of his search for education, for wisdom, is this search for integration, for identity. And above every other instrument he can use stands the original instrument by which each of us became human: the *communication* of himself to other persons, and theirs to him.

In all of what I have been calling his "life-tasks" or core identities—raising his children to independence and maturity, doing his best with a job or a marriage or a community problem, learning to love and understand the world about him—the adult keeps tripping over ghosts, "lost, and by the wind grieved." What mother's relation to her daughter is unfettered by patterns she knew as daughter to *her* mother? What man's approach to bosses or colleagues, to police and to Government, is uncolored by feelings learned in dealing with his father and his brothers?

What is it that moves us so suddenly in a dramatic performance, in an absorbing novel? I think it is a vision of ourselves, or a fragment of ourselves, and that some of these fragments, seen in projection, can be keys that unlock the profound reservoirs of pain and grief and anger that live beneath the citadel of Self. I think this is some of what Aristotle meant by "the catharsis of pity and terror." But we, with a broader empiricism, see also that the individual, confronting other persons of even momentary importance to him, is confronting himself also in various guises. It is as though each man were in a round room whose walls were narrow strips of mirror, floor to ceiling; wherever he looks, he sees some facet of himself. Some please him, and he likes them; some he hates. With some, he goes on fighting battles, long since lost, believing these new foes but somehow mistaking them for old antagonists.

We have, of course, many ways of discharging our feelings through other people. I remember a small boy who was *not* laughing at a slapstick movie comedy. "That ain't funny," he was protesting "somebody could get hurt." And the adults around him, who had been hurt and feared being hurt and knew people they'd like to hurt, were gasping with laughter at the reassuring spectacle of indestructible people surviving catastrophe without a scar.

You must be wondering whether I am saying that adult education is a job for mental health associations. Well, they are part of the movement too; but it might be more accurate to suggest that *mental health content* has a place among the materials of adult education. I do believe that, in this age, adults must include in their equipment some practiced understanding of dynamic mechanisms. "Psychiatry" is too narrow, "mental health" too broad a term for what I have in mind. "Hygiene" is a rather dated word; but it does remind us of what public health education has done to spread popular understanding of sanitation and germ theories and their meaning for personal hygiene. Teaching "psychiatric principles" has too much resulted in anxiety and guilt; and teaching the names of specific diseases and "complexes" has only resulted in their use as epithets, as names we call other people: "Oh, he's just a paranoid." No, what I would try for is only a kind of sophistication about some common fallacies of *mechanism:* the ability to recognize a displacement of feeling onto an inappropriate object; a projection of our own denied fears onto some other source; an identification or a transference, or the "parataxic distortion" that lets me think another person is something I want him to be so that I can love him or fear him, blind to the fact that he is *not* that. All these common, normal ways of digesting experience and excreting what does not nourish our private drives should be parts of our common knowledge. But this is a digression.

The main line of my argument is that the search for self-knowledge is, according to the best of current empirical understanding, carried on through the process of relating to others and communicating with them (and to ourselves) the sense and feeling of those relationships, the ease and unease, comfort or threat, which accompany our role-performance among them. Unmediated, face-to-face communication of this sort is reserved for therapy; though on a lighter, safer level it can be used for leader development, as we have experimented with it in Baltimore;[4] or in the self-exploration practices of group dynamics.

In general adult education, such a process needs the protective cloak of impersonality—or rather third-personality, which is somewhat different. The most familiar form of this is in the group reading plays, novels, biographies, history, or anthropological accounts of other cultures than our own. The same cloak of third-personality is present when we discuss Jefferson, or the United States Supreme Court. The point is that wherever people in a group are talking about other persons, we have to know that they are also, in part, talking about themselves. This, after all, is what makes the group interesting to them. But there are conditions, also pretty well empirically known, which make this process more and less useful to the adult in search of himself.

Because the one-shot lecture or book review does not *involve* the individual sufficiently, it is increasingly being abandoned in the more carefully planned programs of study—in parent education, for example. The minimum requirements for effective learning about oneself are the presence of a peer group, and the continuance of that group long enough so that each member comes to have a *stake* in his relations with the other members. The next requirement is leadership that recognizes the sensitiveness of this situation, and that can create enough security, enough confidence, in the group to enable the members to reveal themselves without having to withdraw from the group in consequence.

[4] See John W. Powell, "Process Analysis as Content: A Suggested Basis for Group Classification," *Journal of Social Issues*, 8, 1952, pp. 54–64.

The optimal method adds the presence of books or other *content* involving the projection of *personalities,* by which the members can mediate and impersonalize—excuse me, *third*-personalize—their own search. Even an abstract work can do this if the group is permitted to stay with it long enough so that the *author* can become a person, a member of the group, though *in absentia.*

What the novelist has projected into his *dramatis personae* comes alive by the group's identification of member with member and of member with character: both are necessary. Let me add the story of a woman in a reading-discussion group who entertained the group at first by "throwing off" on her husband as a lazy lout who wouldn't accept a promotion because he liked the fellows he was working with; wouldn't fight with a man whose car bumped his because the other car was banged up too. She was appealing to the group to affirm her disapproval of him as a man. When we got to Ruth Benedict's account of Zuni life, with its peaceable unaggressive level on which the aggressive individual was a sick deviant, the wife tried tentatively identifying her husband with the Zuni, whom the group approved: "Maybe he should have been an Indian; maybe that isn't a bad way to be." Later still, discussing Epictetus' doctrine that one should worry only about what is within his own control, she tried another view of her husband: maybe he was doing what Epictetus said (and what the group again approved). At the end of the group, she bought an expensive edition of Epictetus—and took it home for her husband.

So what? Well, here was an individual frankly using the group and its materials to practice new ways of looking at one of the chief problem figures in her life. She also enjoyed the group, and it enjoyed her; I think there were many other values beside the one that she made most use of. I single that one out to illustrate why I think we have real evidence that the discussion of dramatic material in groups has genuine valence for adult men and women, genuine power to help them identify their own problems and to get the time, the support, the "withdrawal" (in Toynbee's sense) needed to mobilize the strength and the wit and the understanding to handle them in fresh and creative ways. This is catharsis *plus*.

Let me try your patience with one more story. This concerns a young man whom we shall call Mr. Dorcas. He was a thin and pleasant young man with a detached and supercilious air. His confidence had failed in college after some setbacks; he had subsequently held several jobs and lost them through bad relations with his employers. He was unemployed; and because of impotence, he was faced with failure in his marriage as well. Mr. Dorcas had tried group therapy and lasted three meetings. He had reacted with most tension to topics concerning responsibility for weakness. He had talked in terms of heredity, and of the determination of habits by circumstance. When the third meeting got onto the question of personal responsibility, he quit.

A little later, he joined a reading group. It started with *The Declaration of Independence*. Dorcas maintained that rights were only what a man was strong enough to grab and hold for himself. We went on to *Studs Lonigan:* Dorcas held that character is completely the result of circumstance, and the individual can do nothing about it. Discussing *Patterns of Culture,* he found himself arguing that other cultures didn't "make sense"; and their members should change them—alter the circumstances that had "made" them. With *Look Homeward, Angel,* Dorcas began saying that Eugene Gant's behavior was "crazy," not that it was "determined": Eugene must have been neurotic to do things on impulse that other people wouldn't understand. Dorcas, in other words, was beginning to accept the fact of neurotic illness. Finally, after a bout with Epictetus, we came on Saint Augustine, whose mother, like Lonigan's, wanted him to be a saint, but who made it where Studs didn't. Dorcas started by saying he was puzzled about how much a person controls his own character: "Say, a criminal—what's going to change him into a good man? Maybe he's already gone too far, and not through his own fault." Testing his logic, I asked, "Do you mean one set of circumstances made him what he *is*, but another can't change him back?" Dorcas said, "No, but it would have to be something awfully . . . different . . . it would have to be something he needed *inside* of him." The group argued this; and Dorcas tried going whole hog: "Whatever you are or do, what's happened to you makes you *take the decision* to be or do that. . . . No man can be blamed for what he's doing." This thesis the group rejected in favor of its antithesis, personal responsibility.

Then, finally, hesitantly, Dorcas reached his synthesis: "Y'know, that makes me think, if you want to be good— if you're bad and want to become good—you have to seek the environment that could make you good. . . . You have to *seek the circumstances* that'll help you move in that direction. . . . If you continue, as most people do, just hoping you're going to change, nothing will happen." In that same week, Dorcas re-entered therapy.

Now, this last illustration reveals more fully the way such a group works on its members. I cite it for three reasons: first, it shows a relation between a person's *latent, hidden,* problems, and the manifest verbal discussion in even a nontherapeutic reading group. Second, it says that the interaction of several people over a succession of narratives—novels, anthropological field accounts, autobiography and anecdote—furnished the context in which the latent problem was manifestly solved. And third, it says that the latent problem itself was never mentioned, even while it was being solved.

To do that, however, required time: time, and a situation, in which the members of the group could come to have *something at stake*, some stake in each other, something to win and something to lose; time in which each member could come to feel The Group as an entity, himself as someone related to that entity, and the others as people connected by interaction with each other, with him, and with The Group—which George Mead called the "generalized Other."

I have been laying perhaps too heavy emphasis on reading materials as vehicles for self-illumination, and if so, I plead only that most of my own experience has been with the reading-discussion method. But the same thesis can be illustrated in other forms of adult group activity. *Role playing*, a group technique coming into steadily wider use, and studied intensively by the leaders of the group dynamics movement, is in effect an explicit invitation to lay aside the habituated "person" and release another, latent person that is partly a projection of the imagination and partly a realization of perspectives to which the role player had been paying little heed.

Another revelation of group dynamics has been the many-sidedness of each member's roles within a group: each manifests some aspects of "leadership," even to covertly competing with the leader for the group's allegiance, or sometimes "over-helping" the leader to the group's undoing. A given member may be helpful when A is obstructing, but obstructive when B is trying to forward the group's movement. The major principle of the group dynamics approach is simply that as members are helped to become *aware* of the role they are playing, and of at least part of their motivation, the whole process is freed to move ahead, and the members thereby gain more freedom to realize their constructive social goals as persons.

Further, it is in more than just self-discovery that the group process shows its effectiveness. The work of Lewin and Bavelas, which I mentioned earlier, demonstrated that decisions reached by group members in their groups proved many times as lasting as any acquiescence gained from lectures and movies. The whole moral, then, comes back to the point with which we started: that the essential learning is a changing of response to myself, to other people, and to events, learned in company with others to whom I have so related myself that I care about what I am, what I do, first as one of them, and later after I have left them.

At this point, I believe that what I am trying to say is further supported by a point made by Kenneth Benne in his presidential address to the 1955 AEA Conference: "Our kind of changing society leads continually to the *alienation* of persons and groups from full and living participation in the life of their society and their communities. . . . I would like to say that the major task of adult education is the *reduction of alienation* in our society. If we don't, we are institutionalizing conflict and nonproductive hostility in our communities. . . . So it seems to me that adult educators must become students of human personality. We shall have to recognize and deal with factors deeply embedded in the experience of alienated individuals and . . . in the disorganization of our communities." [5]

Separation of specialized roles and interests, fractioning the self into selves, and alienating persons from their society and from themselves: these describe the problem, the obstacles. But what I have been trying to say in addition is this: that somewhere, almost lost in this language of the psychiatrist and the sociologist, there is a person striving to "find himself," to relate himself to his community and to his society. Our task is dual: to recognize the obstacles, the divisive forces; *and* to recognize the urgent

[5] Kenneth Benne, "Why I Ran for President of AEA," *Adult Leadership*, IV, 7, January, 1956.

underlying drive of the person himself. Adult education is *not* "therapy." The integrating urge is *there*, in the mature individual. Our job is to recognize it, to release it, to give it opportunity and strength and the materials and occasions by which it can make itself effective.

I have said, elsewhere, that we must approach the adult student not as a patient, a victim of events, but as an *agent* of purposes and a performer of functions. We must remember that his own life is the arena for his action; and that the group can best serve as a place of withdrawal, a place to consider the meaning of his other activities. I add, now, that that is what groups *are* doing, no matter what they seem to be talking about. Listen to a group of mothers discussing Studs Lonigan's mother; they criticize, they defend, they analyze and analogize. Above all, they *differ*. If they didn't, the subject would have no interest and no utility for them: this is so, and significant. But listen closely and you will hear what they are really doing: explaining themselves as mothers, defending themselves, attacking or defending their own mothers. They are, as Kant (or Sartre) would say, "legislating" for all mothers, and so their talk is philosophers' talk in its generality. But they are also asking, "Am I good in my role as mother? How do others make out? What can I do instead of what I am doing? Is it my fault the children aren't what I would have them be?" And so their talk is personal talk; but it is mostly in the third person.

A ponderous Georgia Negro millworker in a "criminal psychotic" group at Saint Elizabeth's summed up what I have tried to say, with the piercing insight characteristic of the schizophrenic. We'll call him Mr. James, and on the ward day-room he was quite out of communication—except to ask the doctor for a remedy for the improbable behavior of his perhaps unprecedented intestines, which poured acid into his ears. In the group, he became the philosopher of law. The members had a way of saying "they" do such and such: they put us in here, they could send you to jail. Finally one young man demanded of another, "Why you say 'they' all the time? Who are 'they'?" "We," said Mr. James with slow emphasis. "They is We, everywhere, and all the time. *He* says 'they' because that leaves himself out."

I wanted to call this chapter "They is We." I also thought of borrowing a title from Mr. James' predecessor in philosophy who said, "Ye are all members, one of another." And while I am quoting, let me not omit a wise British group leader, Dr. S. H. Foulkes, who wrote that in the group, the individual is "brought into a situation which he himself is continuously helping to create. . . . He is forced to come out into the open with his reactions, and their contradictions. He meets himself in the situation, projects his own personality and phantasies into it . . . nor can he help facing the others . . . in whom he sees himself as in a mirror" where "the one manifestly displays, personifies, what is suppressed in the other's potential." [6]

In a word, we do *alter* the world as we see it by putting ourselves into dynamic personal relationship to it. This can be "distortion"; or it can be creative. The utmost goal in the search for wisdom is *to become visible to ourselves*. This we can do only in the mirrors of our friends or enemies, of dramatic characters and artistic projections: by truly creative, that is *self*-creative, perception.

I believe that this process of seeing ourselves in other people, and watching them or listening to them for clues to the evaluation of our own modes of relationship behavior, goes on most of the time in most people. There

[6] S. H. Foulkes, *Introduction to Group-Analytic Psychotherapy* (New York: Grune & Stratton, 1949), pp. 61, 70–71. This book was published in collaboration with William Heinemann (Medical Books) Ltd., London.

are a few almost perfectly integrated individuals who look clearly out from a stabilized base of self-acceptance. But the rest of us struggle along amid role-conflicts and self-confusions; we look for cues in others, and find strength in groups to try out being someone we'd like to be. A revealing remark that is sometimes made by people in a reading group is, "I like to be in the group because *I like myself there.*"

The discussion group based on material by or about individuals whose personality or problem is projected with a high valence for the group, or about problems which have personal "role" significance to ourselves, is the perfect instrument for mature learning. Its form recognizes, and meets, the need: it is itself the dramatization of what is within the individual. The individual *is* a group; the group is therefore the most involving and rewarding extension of his own conversation with himself. He comes to it with his feelings and talks in it about his ideas. To disregard either is to fail of educational vitality. Let my last quotation be from myself, with the sanction of two co-authors from other disciplines of instruction: "It is, if you like, precisely *because* man's emotions and his judgments are interwoven that such groups are effective; perhaps, even, that learning in its most vital sense is possible at all." [7]

Where, then, is all this being attempted in adult programs? In more ways than you think: in parent education; in reading groups; in mental health groups; in some leader-development groups; in co-ordinated courses; in odd spots such as "remedial reading"; in residence centers; in group dynamics workshops; and, to an extent, in "human relations" groups in industry. It is happening, without notice, in scores of other groups across the coun-

[7] John Walker Powell, Anthony R. Stone, and Jerome D. Frank, "Group Reading and Group Therapy—A Concurrent Test," *Psychiatry,* 15, 1952, pp. 33–51.

try. My plea, in this chapter, is a special one. It is that we in adult education must become aware of, alert to, this intrapersonal aspect of our group processes, and must increasingly take note of, and plan for, these values in adult discussion. Among all the values of adult group practice, this is the core, this is the most intimate and rewarding *source of learning* for maturity.

Part Four

TOWARD A STRUCTURE FOR
ADULT EDUCATION

CHAPTER 12 *Suggests the Need for Structure*

It takes all the running you can do, to keep in the same place.
—The White Queen

"THERE IS one principal and as it were radical distinction between different minds," observed Francis Bacon, "which is this: that some minds are stronger and apter to mark the differences of things, others to mark their resemblances."

The first mind is happy with the disorderly variegation of the world as it is, and distrusts generalization. To it, a "general principle" or abstraction like "democracy" is just a word with no actual referent; there are actual local democratic practices, which differ from one event to another, but the generality is just a *name*. For this reason these people were called "Nominalists," in the Middle Ages. The other mind feels that the confusion of actual events is uncomfortable, if not downright immoral, and makes no sense until each is brought into some coherent perspective, some synthesis, some sound relationship with other things with which it has *real* identity. So these people were called "Realists." And the controversy between Nominalism and Realism is as vigorous today in adult education as it was among the philosophers from the ninth to the seventeenth centuries.

It must be abundantly clear to you, by now, where my own sympathies tend. I keep speaking of adult learning as a "field," as a "movement" that is growing toward a recognizable pattern based on real, common values and methods, through the convergence of newer methods and more commonly accepted goals and standards. And now I have the temerity to suggest a "structure" for the field. But, though I speak with the tongues of hundreds of my colleagues, I know there are thousands more who resist this language and find it discomforting.

I have to warn them, then, that I shall take a "hard," as against a "soft," position on some of the most controversial issues of our growth as a movement: on the need for a stable institutional form, for a recognizable profession, for a secure and lavish draft upon society's funds. I don't think this is just a matter of personal predilection or unconscious motivation, however. I think the history of other movements and other professions offers some predictive guides to our own. And I believe that we are under not an absolute but a *conditional* necessity to move in these directions: that is, that *unless* we do we shall see history taken out of our hands and made prey to the very forces we ourselves—however disparately—are already committed to combat.

The search for maturity through mental effort, which is our common concern, does not exist in a historical vacuum. It is taking place under perhaps the most destructive stresses that have afflicted a civilization since the breakup of the Roman Empire. The very magnitude of our hopes for new achievement through new tools and forces is overmatched by our terror of those forces themselves. We are alternately hurtled into public concerns and repelled into private retreats. We are very rich, and very much afraid. We fear an enemy abroad, but also fear to let ourselves study his real nature, and resent any inquiry into our stereotypes about him. Only yesterday

we were on the brink of a moral collapse of our own democracy; and the gravest symptom of it was our fear of
asking each other the very questions that had to be asked
if we were to identify the source of our peril. The
precious word "freedom" has itself become an article of
dogma, though we know it perishes with our right to
question its meaning and existence.

We are paying ourselves, to be lulled and diverted,
thousands of times what we spend to acquire alertness
and understanding. We are pouring oceans of energy into
engineering invention; but those are few who believe
that educational invention will be rewarded by an equal
outpouring of mental energy by our own people.

Against this threatened erosion of America's mind and
spirit, against this looming dust bowl of abandoned leadership, we propose to pit the green thumb of learning.
We call for a renaissance of free inquiry, of curiosity and
creativeness and comprehension. With what hope?

"Adult education," librarian Nettie Taylor of Maryland's
Library Extension Service once remarked, "is a state of
mind." This is, I think, probably the basic truth about it.
Its motivation, in those who have devoted themselves to
it, is a strange mixture of feelings. Impatience and com-
passion, so beautifully illustrated in Mr. Pockheel and
H✶Y✶M✶A✶N K✶A✶P✶L✶A✶N; enthusiasm and frustration;
a vision and a shrug. I remember once complaining to
Dr. Meiklejohn that it was like rowing upstream against
a heavy current; no matter how hard you row, the land-
marks on the shore never change. "Yes," he said, "but think
where we'd be if we stopped rowing."

In practice, education is *my* attempt to get you to do
something that I believe in and believe you will believe
in when you do it. On the "demand" side, it may be *your*
attempt to get me to do something for you, which I
may or may not quite approve of. The attempt to meet demand has always operated somewhat against the educator's

own preferences, so that both parties end up being a trifle wistful.

So the importance of identifying the strongly emerging trends is just that these must be the points on which demanders and suppliers have come to agree. From these trends we can infer future directions; and on them we can build with new and greater energy and unanimity and boldness.

We shall have to be very bold indeed to match the weight of history that presses us backward. And as any student of stresses can tell us, the resistance to stress is what creates structure. Sheer pressure, without man's intervention, can crystallize carbon into coal or diamonds. But man invented the structured diversion of thrust; and created architecture.

Of course, by remaining fluid and separate, like water or sand, thrust can be let pass harmlessly by. But we in our movement have gone beyond that point. We are inescapably on the path that leads to architectural organization: fluid and mobile, perhaps, never monolithic and static; but there will be structure. Our task right now, therefore, is to begin exploring the principles of an architecture for adult education.

The elements of such a structure have been repeatedly described in recent literature. For the sake of continuity, let me quote from a book in which, in 1949, I asked myself the questions that the present book is trying to answer.

"In the training of children and young people, in the training of young adults for trades and professions, our culture has developed familiar institutions. Here one speaks confidently of the School, the College, the University, or of the Medical School, the Military Academy, the Music Conservatory. But America has found no School, in that sense, for adults. For the vocations of grown men and women we do provide; but for the vocation of maturity itself we are at a loss.

"Among the thousands of adult agencies, there is no established form. . . . Among the myriad courses, there is no field of studies, no area of inquiry that could be called the 'adult curriculum'; nor any body of materials. . . . And at the center of our confusion, there is no guiding concept of the adult himself, or of his mind and purpose, from which the pattern of a school could be derived.

"When a boy studies to become an engineer, his teachers know what he must learn to do. But . . . is there a subject field, a career discipline of the mind, whose content and method are implicit in the concept of maturity? The law school, the medical school, even the children's school, are bound by goals and standards set and sanctioned by the members of a profession. What profession sets the goals and enforces the standards of an education for maturity?"[1]

A school and profession whose form and functions are drawn from the implications of maturity itself, and integrated into the governing structure of the democratic community; a profession "capable of attracting *and supporting* an adequate corps of full-time leaders": If we face these needs seriously, what structural outlines suggest themselves?

[1] John Walker Powell, *Education for Maturity* (New York: Hermitage Press, 1949), pp. 32–33.

CHAPTER 13 *Suggests Some Institutional Patterns*

> And give . . .
> A local habitation and a name.
> —Shakespeare

THE ENDLESS VARIETY of institutional patterns—of affiliation, staffing, programming—has been both the pride and the weakness of the adult learning movement. It has allowed free play to the *genius loci*; and it has hampered the development of standards of competence. No program is answerable for anything save the reputation it can assert for itself. Agency does not compare program with agency, or locality with locality. The consumer takes what he finds.

The statistics of the institutional reports indicate that people of different levels of schooling, achievement, and income vary slightly in the institutions they are willing to attend; with the college graduates (entering the adult world at the rate of about three hundred and fifty thousand a year) tending to go to the colleges and Extension Divisions, or to the independent adult centers that offer the greatest intellectual challenge, or else to the adult activity associations that offer programs of action.

People go, and will continue to go, to schools and colleges for classes and workshops and groups; to libraries for books and records and films, and sometimes discussions;

190

extension courses will continue to come to them. Shops and unions will go on offering learning. Rural groups will continue to get service from home demonstration agents and county agents and 4-H workers and the rest. And so on, through the catalog of learning leadership. But in every case, as I have already remarked, they will be getting the secondary attention of agencies whose primary job is with something else; with youth, with print, with wages, with improving farm incomes.

And by "secondary" I mean more than just that the agency was developed for another purpose. Its most practical meaning is shown whenever population pressures or financial pressures begin to bear down. Then it is the secondary, the adult, program that suffers. Many colleges have recently said they were cutting down their adult programs because of the pressures of a growing undergraduate population on staff, buildings, and budget. A recent Maryland survey found at least twice as many high school graduates qualified to go to college as were actually going; and proposed steps to bring more of them on to college levels. I would suppose this situation was true for the nation, and ways will be found to increase the proportion of college-goers—but at the expense of adult community services by the colleges. School systems with full-time adult administrators are very much in the minority among our cities and towns; even our states are not uniform in this respect. And where the responsibilities are divided between the needs of children and of adults, the huge wave of oncoming children is likely to wash away much of the attention to adult programs. Libraries under financial and population pressures have to fall back to their original job; lack of staff and of the head librarian's attention were most often given as reasons why libraries were *not* carrying on adult programs they would have liked to offer. The wider use of extramural facilities can avoid the competition for classrooms; and fuller employment of adult-level personnel will lessen the pressure on faculties. But this will require devotion to the adult learning goals, including diversion of funds. And this, I believe, will be best sustained if there is a stable, recognized, and superior institution which can maintain leadership of the movement in each state.

What is needed, therefore, is *an agency primarily and uniquely adult, independent of other concerns, staffed by its own profession and financed purely for what it is and does.*

Second, it must stand at the top of the learning ladder, from where it can reach back as far as necessary—even to the beginnings of literacy—but where its students will not pass on beyond it and out of its reach.

This position was foreshadowed in the report of the President's Commission on Higher Education in 1947, from which Grattan summarizes two major recommendations: first, "that the suggested ends of adult education should be accepted by the colleges and universities as a justification of their support in a democratic society. The Commission insisted that *all* institutions of higher education should in some degree become community institutions" to the extent of spending "one hundred million dollars a year in the future on adult education." Second, and very important, the Commission added that *new machinery* was needed at state and national levels, for "continuous studies of adult ... needs and interests, the training of teachers and leaders, the preparation of instructional materials, the evaluation of what is going on, the stimulation of experimentation in instructional methods and subject matters, and the stimulation of constant expansion"—with federal financial aid.[1]

What I would add is that the "new machinery" must be exempt from competition with the old, from the risk of

[1] C. Hartley Grattan, *In Quest of Knowledge* (New York: Association Press, 1955), pp. 292–293.

divided attention, divided allegiance, divided administration. For this reason, the University Extension, for example, would not qualify. A few adventurous divisions, in places such as Madison, Minneapolis, Lafayette, Los Angeles, are reaching ahead into fully adult services with one hand; but the other is tied behind them by the need to offer undergraduate instruction off campus.

Now: what clues can we find in current adult educational practice that point in the direction of our search?

First, I would cite the trend toward *resident adult centers* on such campuses as Minnesota and Michigan State, with Wisconsin's, Purdue's and Georgia's still a-building. These centers house all manner of institutes, short courses, conferences, in or out of residence. There is a new and definite trend toward a short-term structure for adult programs, and with a preference for common residence where that is possible. A week end, a week or two in the vacation months, fit easily into normal adult rhythms. Colleges and folk schools—Goddard, for example, or the Highlander Folk School—have for years found it profitable to invite adult students into short-term residence. Even back in the thirties, the School of Social Studies and Mills College used to team up in a yearly trans-Bay partnership for a Seminar-in-Residence on the Mills campus. Starr reports that labor education is showing this same trend toward week-end and short-term structure, as preferable to the once-a-week-for-ten-weeks schedule. And Powell's Second Law holds that the effectiveness of the group relationship grows as the square of the frequency of meetings: meeting once a week, the process takes hold four times as fast as with meetings every two weeks; and three to fourteen days in a row, with the added advantage of common meals and recreation, produce proportionately greater results in less time.

The campus adult centers are kept very full and very busy, by all accounts. Because the scheduling of meetings and rooms for all sorts of groups from across a state is a very complicated business, the manager of a center is more a hotel manager than an educator; the center is simply a *facility* that adult students and leaders make use of. But its existence makes possible a variety of important occasions which it would be very difficult to house without a center. This, then, I take as one important clue to our problem.

Another may emerge from the consideration of some experiences from the FAE's "Test Cities" and Test Centers. Several of these have been experimenting with methods of affiliation, of financing, and of program promotion; and usually no two in quite the same way. Of the Test Cities, let's look at three.

Chattanooga chose to set up an Adult Education Council that would not only bring all adult agencies together but would also sponsor its own discussion courses, lectures, leader-training institutes, and even TV programs. The emphasis was on the major areas of public and foreign affairs, family life, including attention to "senior citizens," economics, and the humanities. Funded on a decreasing scale over three years, but with the addition of special supplementary grants from both FAE and the Foreign Policy Association, the Council had increased its local contributions to around ten thousand dollars in 1954–55, against a budget of more than twenty-five thousand. With a staff of three, and seven volunteer committees, the Council has undertaken the task of pulling together all the city's resources for liberal education. It is not clear what its relation is to the local University, which is at least a member of the Council. The pattern here, then, is not very different from that of some earlier Councils, or the Dallas Civic Federation: an independent organization running its own program and hoping for financial support from the citizens, but needing subsidies too. In the words of George Connor, the Council's executive, "an educational organization cannot make an emotional appeal" for funds, and so must rely on the social and educational convictions of those who hold such convictions: never the strongest lever for prying up money.

San Bernardino followed another pattern. Here an adult center for liberal studies was grafted on to the local Junior College, with the latter's enthusiastic assent. The program has made a wide impact through the hearty collaboration of radio and press; and the costs are being assumed by the College, at the end of the three-year test period covered by the FAE grant.

Akron took another tack. After an initial flirtation with the city's University, the program was independently embodied in an Adult Education Foundation with its own sources of support, and with a "senate" consisting of a board of directors and a "house" organized as a city-wide Adult Education Council. The third phase saw the director taken into the University, but with the Foundation and Council still independently operating and self-financed. The University also offers an adult program and has had success with a new program of late-afternoon classes for interested women. What the ultimate integration of the University's program and the Foundation's will be, I cannot yet tell. But here is at least the pattern of an independent adult program operating with university backing and identity.

The several local Test Centers recently set going by the FAE have not had time really to demonstrate their potential. At this writing, they have not yet been freed to undertake educational planning on their own, or even to make use of educational offerings other than those approved by the Fund. In all but one case, these centers are affiliated with local colleges and universities; but they are expected to come as close as possible to paying their own way through the promotion of fee-paying co-ordinated courses. Curiously, though the FAE supports both Great

Books and the Foundation for Political Education's reading courses, administrative differences over standard fee requirements have limited the use of their materials by the Test Centers. These limitations are natural concomitants of a trial period. The question one is left with is: When does the "testing" end and a secure operation begin? In theory, after four years of trial. But the Fund itself cannot foretell the future until the parent Ford Foundation has achieved a clearer policy toward the children's allowance. At present, the grant supporting the Fund runs for five years only.

Now, if we follow these signposts, where do we come out?

On the state level, we come out with an Adult Center backed by the resources and prestige of a university; but we would staff it with the members of an adult learning profession: not members of a "Department" or an Extension Division, but members of *an adult arm independent of the undergraduate responsibilities* of the institution. They are men and women adept in the arts, the sciences, the social sciences, the Big Discourse of civilization; among them are people alert to the issues of Law, of Government, of Democracy; and people skilled in helping the citizens of a community identify and take arms against their own sea of troubles. There are skills in group dynamics, in discussion, in the literature of adult learning. There are resources of books, film, tape, records, microfilm, radio, television; and there is a solid recognition of the adult value of air-conditioning, of chairs and tables, paper and pencil, blackboard and chalk, of projectors, tape and record players, of acoustics and comfort: the tools of the twentieth century to serve the Enlightenment of man.

On the local level, we appear to have a choice: a Center to which all agencies and organizations may turn for professional help; or a professionally staffed Council that, while pulling together the adult resources of the town, also creates and sponsors its own programs, and helps other agencies upgrade theirs.

The training of the professionals, however, raises new problems. A person learns, essentially, not *what* he is taught but *how* he is taught. The graduates of a graduate school learn not adult education but graduate-school education; and this is not appropriate to *adult* learning. The training must itself be carried on in fully adult ways, in a truly adult center. So our State Center is the training center, also.

Ideally, one would suppose that the local centers or Council offices would be locally supported and governed, but at the same time would be outposts, so to speak, of the State Center. In the latter, program would be developed out of national source materials, and adapted to the needs and character of the state. From it would go—and to it, come—the people who spend their lives in learning about, and from, and among, other adult learners and doers: that is, the potential members of the profession. The State Center would function partly as campus resident centers do now, and partly as the Faculty of Adult Studies. To the Center would come institute and workshop and program groups of organization leaders and community leaders; from it would go trainees into internships in local organizations, into labor programs and factories, into rural programs, into libraries and evening schools and social agencies. To it would come librarians and community college and Agricultural Extension and evening school staff, for short-term in-service development. In the local community, the graduates would find positions *as* adult educators with skills to serve agencies and organizations; or they would go into library schools, and the training academies of other professions. And the local pool of educated leaders would grow steadily larger.

Standardization? No; we know the answers to that one: local coloring of interest and need; personal differences of special interest and skill; and the undergirding values of creative curiosity and the liberation of the minds of individual men and women.

To realize such a dream, our universities would have to learn how to relinquish traditional controls, and devise new forms of affiliation to give sanction and support. Our towns, and the agencies within them, would have to learn how to accept a genuine *community of interest* while still cherishing their local "personality." Our national organizations would have to learn that their vitality is in their local units, and that the strength of each of these is drawn from sources within its own community. And all of us, as we gradually came to recognize ourselves in this new pattern, would at last have the chance to begin learning more fully from each other.

To preserve the energy and color of community and agency programs, and still follow the big score with our separate instruments; to follow the lead of a conductor without forgetting that it is the audience that must make the music: this is the orchestration of adult learning.

CHAPTER **14** *Proposes a Profession*

> Professions first appear as customary activities largely modified by detached strains of theory. . . . The older professional practice was rooted upon custom, though it was turning toward the intellectual sunlight.
>
> —A. N. Whitehead,
> *Adventures of Ideas*

HERE IS the most curious and most revealing fact about adult education as an occupation: When people come to us and say, "I'd like to work in adult education. Where do I start?" the only thing we can say is, "Become something else, and after you've done that perhaps you can do a bit of this." To enter a *career* in adult education, you can start by learning to be a librarian, an agricultural or farm-life expert, an administrator; you can learn a trade and join a union and become expert in labor organization, history, and practice; you can get a job in industry and work toward the training division; you might go into the ministry, or the army; you might train for social work, for psychiatry, for geriatrics; you might go to New York and apply for a job in some special-interest organization—mental health, political reform, interfaith or interracial work, whatever you had training for; you could look for a job in radio or television; you could even train for school or college teaching. *Then,* after you were established in a

199

job that had its own goals and demands and duties, you might undertake to divert some, or even all, of your time to the adult-teaching phases of the position. The positive side, of course, is that you may in this way come to master a field of knowledge which is needed in adult learning. The negative is that you will not in this way learn it in adult terms, or in its relevance to the dynamic needs of an adult community.

You can also turn to several University Departments of Education for training in this field—preferably after you have your job; if you get the training first, even up to the doctor's degree, there are relatively few places you can get a job as just an adult educator: mostly in public school program administration or in Agricultural Extension.

Svenson[1] in 1953–54 found a total of fifty-three institutions offering some work in adult education, ranging from summer institutes in residence to organized curricular offerings leading to an M.A. or a Ph.D. Columbia, New York University, and Chicago were the early pioneers, in the thirties; seven other universities have seriously undertaken planned graduate and undergraduate work in this field since World War II. Usually, the total amount of faculty time devoted to these courses totals less than the equivalent of two full-time positions. Course offerings often grow out of the customary Education Department emphases on administration, program planning, finance and promotion; adult psychology and the history of adult education are standard; leader-training is sometimes included; and most of the twelve major universities working at this job offer some chance for observation of actual adult agencies; some even provide working experience, paid or unpaid, within adult agencies. At least a dozen other colleges offer one or two courses in adult education, or accept related courses

[1] Elwin V. Svenson, *Professional Preparation Programs for Leaders in Adult Education,* unpublished thesis, University of California at Los Angeles, 1954.

for credit toward the education degree with an adult emphasis. There are, *in total,* ten professors of adult education now on university faculties in this country.

For part-time volunteers and lay leaders, the opportunities for short-term training are growing rapidly; over fifty workshops, institutes, and short courses were offered in the summer of 1955. But the bulk of leader-development is probably still being done by the organizations within which these people expect to serve. Lois McCarthy's summary of the report on the Council of National Organizations remarks, "It is significant that the largest part of the training is given in and by the organization rather than by or in co-operation with outside organizations. . . . Is this because recognized educational institutions have not met a particular need on teaching methods for the type of group represented in the Council? Or is orientation to the organization's point of view the main emphasis? . . . It may well be that this general inadequacy of training programs for those who teach adults is reflected in the findings on professional standards"—which are that "lack of [professional] standards and training . . . are two of their largest problems."

This complaint can be matched by nearly all the FAE studies. Here is Loomis: "All leaders involved in adult education in rural America need professional training and experience in rural life, the social sciences, and adult education. Such training should be of professional level and coupled with in-service training. Relatively few leaders are sufficiently trained in these fields." The Library study concluded: "The most urgent [finding] is the need for education and training. . . . It is essential to gain the necessary education, training, and experience in the knowledge and skills needed for the successful carrying out of adult education responsibilities . . . but the library schools are offering very little in the philosophy of adult education and less in the skills needed to conduct a program." The Public Schools study "clearly indicates that there is a need for more teachers of adults" and that "teachers of adults need additional training." The University Extension study points out that experts in adult education alone are unusable by Extension Divisions, but so are subject experts without professional training in working with adults. The needs of both management and labor for professional help, guidance, and training are obvious. And so on to infinity.

Add it up, and this is the sum: All manner of agencies, institutions, and associations are engaged in promoting learning activities among adults. All of them are crying for professional training and assistance. And there is no profession.

What *is* a profession? Many scholars have proposed criteria. Let me offer mine:

1. A profession is a recognized and distinguishable discipline of learning, skill, research, and practice, in a service useful to society.
2. Its philosophy, content, and techniques are communicable through teaching.
3. Its roots of learning, training, and research are on the university level, and capable of recognition in the form of advanced graduate degrees.
4. Its practice tends toward the conservation and promotion of values explicitly cherished by the society within which it operates.
5. Its members are self-governing within their profession, and have control over standards of training, entrance, and performance; and maintain ethical standards among themselves.
6. Its practitioners command salaries commensurate with those of other professions requiring equivalent training.
7. Its practice has authorized and publicly recognized relationships to related and to ancillary professions,

to lay activities in its field, and to volunteer services by lay people.

Test these against, say, the profession of medicine. The only one that may not seem clear is number seven. This means that doctors stand in a clearly known relationship to, say, public health professionals; to graduate nurses, practical nurses, aides, orderlies; to health associations; and to volunteer home or hospital workers. Now, in addition, remember the great variety of specialties within the profession of medicine: a psychiatrist need not be a surgeon, a pediatrician does not practice geriatrics, a research specialist might not practice at all. And of course a hospital administrator need not be a medical man.

Now consider what these criteria would mean for adult education:

1. *A profession is a recognized and distinguishable discipline of learning, skill, research, and practice, in a service useful to society.*

The ten professors of adult education, meeting at the national conference in 1955, agreed that they could not agree on a distinct body of subject matter for their field, and gave themselves five years to find one. But Howard McClusky, one of their number, said from the platform that we now have enough knowledge of methods, of adult psychology, of the social science of groups and communities, to solidify a body of knowledge around which a profession could be formed. Our own survey, in this book, has suggested that there is substantial and growing agreement about the nature of adult needs, the values of group method, the varieties of learning situations, the dynamics of interpersonal relationship, the techniques of community intervention, and the methods for leadership preparation. The literature of adult education is becoming constantly more adult, more focused; and research, on both graduate and project levels, is increasing steadily. It investigates method, evaluation techniques, content, training, institutional roles, community effects, expectations and values. The Committee on Social Philosophy and Direction Finding of the Adult Education Association persists in trying to set going a continual "philosophizing" about goals and values and ethics, among not only the membership but among their local friends and associates. The annual conferences of the Association have focused on content and target goals: world awareness in 1954, community action in 1955, individual goals in 1956.

On the other hand, these same conferences have revealed sharp cleavages within the practicing membership. An appeal to get adults enlisted in "the Big Discourse" of civilization, made by C. Wright Mills at the 1955 conference, was lampooned into "the Big Disgust" by a rural leader, to the applause of several administrators. A threatened split over "community development" and "education" was averted in 1955 by the statesmanlike persuasions of Cyril Houle, Kenneth Benne, and Howard McClusky. Cleavage is inherent in this movement; but the role of the true professional is revealed in this sort of statesmanship.

The principal objection to this article of faith, however, has come from independent Adult Center directors who fear that the assertion of a "common subject matter" would mean "standardization of program under Teachers College graduates without any real sense of adult needs," and would "stifle the inventiveness of local individuals and programs." This is a very important objection, and deserves discussion. But first let's explore some of the other criteria as they apply to our field.

   2. *Its philosophy, content, and techniques are communicable through teaching.*

Carl Rogers, in the memorandum already referred to, also says, "My experience has been that I cannot teach another

person how to teach." I know too well what he means;
I have shared the initial despair of leader-development
groups whose members conclude, "This has been a most
enriching experience for me, but I couldn't communicate
to anyone else the real sense of it." The point here is that
the experience of growth and insight is essentially incom-
municable. But this does *not* mean that the *conditions
that produce such experience* cannot be reproduced; and
in fact that is what Rogers and other sophisticated group
leaders do. In a paper on leader development a few years
back I wrote: "If what we want for our mothers' group
members is that they become more sensitively aware of
the ways they relate to their children at home, we must in
the group provide experiences that sensitize their awareness of the ways they relate to each other. And the goal,
the tone, the mores that lead to this end, have to be set by
a leader who is already sensitive to his own ways of relating to group members, as well as to their ways of relating
with each other. . . . The logic runs in a straight line from
the leader through the group experience to the area of performance of the group's members."[2]

In other words, the techniques of adult leadership are
communicable—if not verbally, then through the provision
for experiences that in turn make the potential leader able
to provide equivalent experiences for his groups. It is primarily the professionally trained and experienced trainer
who is able to do this: whether his training has been in
group dynamics, in mental health, in workshops and institutes, there is a common knowledge and technique that
converges upon this particular skill. Professional literature,
from "workshop" articles in the AEA's *Adult Leadership*
and *Leader's Digests* through manuals like Knowles's *Informal Adult Education,* to the sophisticated instructions
about the discussion leader's job put out by the Center

[2] John W. Powell, "Process Analysis as Content: A Suggested Basis for
Group Classification," *Journal of Social Issues,* 8, 1952, pp. 54–64.

for the Study of Liberal Education for Adults and by the FAE's Experimental Discussion Project, is increasingly alert to, and agreed upon, the dynamics of group behavior and of individual response in groups.

Less commonly communicated are the means of making *content media* useful to adult groups. Most book-discussion leaders in the co-ordinated programs are given a skimpy run-through of part of the material, by the sponsoring organization. The Film Council of America developed and spread abroad a consensus about improved methods of leading film discussions. Eugene Johnson's work in San Bernardino opens encouraging roads to methods of leading home radio-listener discussion.

Because adult learning has the entire world of print and its equivalents to draw upon, it has felt little need for a literature of its own apart from the professional literature of method. In consequence, as I have said, its practitioners can be, and very often are, people who have no knowledge toward which a group's attention can be focused. I believe it is quite essential that we come to focus at least on certain areas of learning with which educated adults *have* to be familiar; and that we insist that adult educators must have developed at least some mastery in one of these areas. The kind of knowledge which is needed is broader than that possessed by course-instructors; the historian, the Latinist, the art expert, the anthropologist, are not yet possessed of the knowledge that will help adults become literate in the broad ranges of their living. At this point, then, we are *not* quite ready to be a profession; for we have in common little to give our leaders but a methodology of conversation; and nothing to ask of our subject-specialists but *expertise*.

The professional in adult education will be an educated person, a generalist of adult concerns and perhaps a specialist in some one of them. He will be this not because he wants a retreat into scholarship, the occupational disease of the collegiate teacher. He will be this because he is moved by a warmth of liking and respect for people, because he is drawn to them and believes in them and in their need and ability to help themselves through their own learning. He will not settle for being, himself, less of a learner than they. His own curiosity will be alive, his creativeness constantly stirred by the uniqueness of the people and situations he meets, his comprehension adequate to the demands of working with his peers. His competence will be primarily in communication, and in helping others communicate among themselves. But he will know materials, in print and otherwise, the way a librarian knows her books; and within some part of that literature, he will have his own motivation to learning.

He will also know the ways of group decision and action; of group motivation to community change and betterment. But even of this there is a literature; and action can lead to study.

All of this must be imbedded in our provisions for *the teaching of adult teachers.* With some of this wisdom, they will help lay volunteers and agency staff members become leaders; and these in turn will help their groups of grownups learn how to learn from each other, how to tackle their problems in concert. But at the source of this spreading delta of education must stand the professional.

The current emphasis is on using the expert at the *source* of program preparation, leaving little need for expertness at the point of use. This is especially clear in the co-ordinated course. But a large number of adult offerings consist of subject courses at college and university levels. What I am here proposing is not quite either of these. The adult education professional knows more about methods and people and their learning needs and the content of that learning than does the university teacher; and he is in closer and more continuous relationship with the using groups than is the expert author of a co-ordinated course. The notion of a local manager-promoter-organizer, as developed by the Experimental Discussion Project, also leaves a good deal to be desired. The educator is more than a salesman of do-it-yourself kits for learning. Unless he himself is fired with interest and tested by some discipline of learning, he will lose interest, and if he succeeds as a promoter, will be hired away by another promoter. He must, I would predict, either rise toward the ability to handle an educational program in creative terms, or sink in a sea of tally sheets and cost accounts.

The educator, the man in charge of the learning efforts of a large body of people, must be one of a company. He has two main tasks: to find ways of inspiring people to learn in company; and to maintain their courage to keep on inquiring into the conditions of their common life. He must enlist them both in the carrying forward of their culture and in the critical questioning of it.[3] For these tasks, neither a remote-control publishing office with local managers nor a body of skilled but unlearned methodologists will be adequate. The development of adult education into a genuine force in our culture requires the development of teachers, teachers of a wholly new order; and they will have to be trained. My comment on the second criterion, therefore, is that the full scope of this profession *can* be communicated through teaching; but *is not* being so at present.

3. *Its roots of learning, training, and research are on the university level, and capable of recognition in the form of advanced graduate degrees.*

[3] "The salvation of the community depends upon those individuals whose education gives them the moral and intellectual strength to stand out when necessary against the majority. *It may be added that such are precisely the men and women for whom an adequate system of adult education should find work to do as teachers.*" *General Education in a Free Society,* Harvard Report, Harvard University Press, 1945, cited by Grattan, p. 290. The italics are his, but have my blessing also.

This criterion immediately involves the one before it: i.e., where and how can such teachers be developed? I assert the university level because that is the highest available institution we have, except for such Advanced Study centers as those at Princeton and Stanford. The university is where every major profession hangs its hat. A high school diploma plus self-teaching and experience are no longer enough. The home of a fully developed adult educational profession will have to be at least of university grade and graduate status.

4. *Its practice tends toward the conservation and promotion of values explicitly cherished by the society within which it operates.*

This would appear to be self-evident; but we can take nothing for granted. What are the values that this profession would serve? Free inquiry; experimental action; study for the enrichment of life, for the increase of adult competency, for the strengthening of civic participation (these were goals 1, 2, 3, in the responses to the Public School adult study); the strengthening of democracy in the family and the town and in national action; the development of individual responsibility, independence, and coherence of purpose and accomplishment. *What other profession serves this pattern of ends?*

5. *Its members are self-governing within their profession, and have control over standards of training, entrance, and performance; and maintain ethical standards among themselves.*

This is the difference between a "profession" and an "association." "The term Profession," writes Alfred North Whitehead, "means an avocation whose activities are subjected to theoretical analysis, and are modified by theoretical conclusions. . . . Thus foresight based upon theory, and theory based upon understanding of the nature of things, are essential to a profession. . . . Perhaps the most important function of these institutions is the supervision of standards of individual professional competence and of professional practice. For this purpose there is a complex interweaving of universities and more specialized institutions. The problem of freedom comes in here. For it is not opinions which are censured, but learning and ability. Thus in the more important fields of thought, opinion is free and so are large divergencies of practice. The community is provided with objective information . . . as to the sort of freedom of action which may safely be granted. Further, even large freedom can now be allowed to non-professional individuals. . . . There can be only one appeal, and this is to the general professional opinion as exhibited in the practice of accredited institutions." [4]

Association means a loose assemblage of memberships among people who share one interest, and possibly no others. It can attract loyalty; it does not command that major portion of a man's identity which is his membership in his profession. If one asks a medical man, "Who are you?" he will answer, "I am a physician." If one asks a faculty man who he is, he may say, "I am a historian." But who among us, when you ask him that question, will answer, "I am a member of the Adult Education Association of the United States of America"?

Association is of great importance. It is what creates communication and a sense of shared purpose and the fruitful exchange of ideas and experiences among those who share some activity in common. It makes visible the fact, and some of the personnel, of our movement—visible to the public as well as to each other. We know we are traveling in company, and we find many friends in that company. An association can publish journals of great

[4] A. N. Whitehead, *Adventures of Ideas* (New York: The Macmillan Co., 1933), pp. 72–78. Used with permission of the publishers.